More Than Once
Round The Block

By

Andy Rosholm-Olesen

*To Shiela,
with love & best wishes,

Andy xxx*

H.I. Bowls Club.

New Generation **Publishing**

I would like to thank my long suffering partner Maggie, who has stoically put up with all my trips down memory lane whilst I have been writing this book. Thanks for your love and understanding.

Chapters

My Story

I don't quite know where to start with this; so perhaps before I was born will show my arrival was unexpected.

My father was a Danish fisherman who had the misfortune to have his boat sunk during the war (2nd World war), on the fortunate side he was picked up by a Russian trawler after being in the freezing water for twenty-one hours. Then deposited in Britain where he was whisked away to an internment camp somewhere in the south while they checked him out to make sure he wasn't a German spy. Having confirmed that he was innocent of any nefarious intent they bundled him off to Fleetwood as they thought he would be more useful in feeding our wartime isle as a fisherman rather than the potatoes picker they were employing him as.

This is where he met my mum and fell for her it wasn't really reciprocated but she thought he was good fun and good mate material, not to mention the fact that her best friend was going out with a Danish chap and she feared when the war was over she would go of to Denmark and leave my mum behind! Best laid plans and all that, the upshot was my mum fell pregnant with me, so she married my dad, her best friend dumped her intended and stayed in Fleetwood while my mum was whisked off to Denmark just before the birth was due, a little ironic to say the least.

Things didn't go well for my mum, she was away from home for the first time ever, couldn't speak or understand the language and desperately missed her mum. My dad showed he had a nasty side, which didn't go down very well; it was so bad that his mother took my mum off to a friend of hers who could speak English and asked my mum if she wanted to go home? She did, so her mother-in-law arranged and paid my mums passage back on a Danish butter boat. I made my entrance into the world on the day she got back to her mum's. Her mum thought I wasn't due to come in to the world till June so thought nothing of dragging my mum to the library with her saying the walk would do her good after being stuck on a boat for three days. I very nearly made my entrance on the top of the library stairs. Fortunately they managed to get home an hour before I was born, maybe that's why I always enjoyed reading!

My first memory of meeting my dad was when I was about three, I was quite taken with this chap who was making such a fuss of me and was talking in a funny voice .My nana who looked after me whilst mum was at work said he was my daddy apart from him taking a lot of interest in my ears I thought he was great (he was checking to make sure I hadn't inherited his mother's very large ears apparently). So when he said he had to go to walk my mum home from work, I said in all innocence "my mummy doesn't need walking home she does it by herself all the time and sometimes she doesn't even come home!" With that he left very rapidly and my nana very white faced and angry shot me off to bed. It was the first time I had ever seen my nana angry. I woke up to lots of shouting and screaming and the finality of a door crashing shut. When I got brave enough to creep downstairs my nana was on her hands and knees mopping blood up from the lino, she was sobbing and screamed at me to get back to bed. When I woke up in the morning it was my dad in bed with me not my mum! What he had done when he left us was go to the hotel where my mum worked behind the bar and glowered at her till closing time then left before she finished and sat waiting in my nanas for her to come home where he laid into her and smashed her face to a pulp. When she came back later that day I didn't recognise her and ran from her. I have never forgotten that day and night when in my innocence I got my mum the beating of her life, the only reason she didn't come home sometimes was because they had late functions at the hotel and the staff stayed over.

I don't know quite how it happened after all the hullabaloo but they ended up back together to try and make a go of it. So my next memory was living in a very large house in Hull, with a huge back garden, we only had a yard at my nanas terraced house with an outside loo! I was playing in the garden when I heard a very posh voice say" look there's a fairy at the bottom of the garden", I was looking for it but they meant me, I was lifted over the fence and made a royal fuss of. It turned out that the family consisted of the mother, her spinster daughter and bachelor twin sons, known to me as Mistress Peggy, Master Harry and Master Alec, so they were seriously posh and took a real shine to me, which was fortunate as I am unable to remember any of the bad stuff that went on in our house between mum and dad. I discovered if I dragged a chair near the front door I could manage to open it and go next door for breakfast, my mum was usually asleep so didn't miss me. All went well until one day they asked what I would like to eat and I said " a careful butty" of course they didn't even know what a butty was never mind a careful one so they woke my mum with a very weepy me in tow to find out what it was! Apparently a syrup sandwich and when mum used to give it to me she said "careful ", mystery solved. Another abiding memory of the time was when I met the second twin, up to then I'd only met Master Harry as they took it in turns working between the UK and Canada something to do with an airline, anyway I was playing in the street and looked up to see Master Harry coming towards me, I ran up to him and threw myself into his arms only to realise there

7

was something different about him I don't know what as they were identical I screamed blue murder, everyone came out and calmed the situation down no doubt having a laugh about it because although he hadn't met me he knew everything about me from his family. He went off to buy me an ice cream to mollify me but being unused to children he made the mistake of buying me a wafer instead of a cornet apparently I was most put out and slammed it through their letter box in a very un-fairy like manner. At some stage we ended up back in Fleetwood at my nanas once more without my dad, all I can remember about the happenings between them then is that it was always in the night I could hear all the shouting and swearing. Our neighbours kept in touch with me for quite a while they used to send me gifts to turn me into a " little lady", like pretty embroidered tray covers and napkins, handkerchiefs and lovely scented soap in the shape of teddy bears, truly delightful people. I think I still have a letter somewhere telling me to grow up into a lovely lady. (Just as well they didn't meet me later on in my life).

Well the next few years were pretty normal, we lived at my nanas, my mum went to work and I was enrolled in infant school then on to primary. It was lovely being with my nana who I adored; my life was filled with fairy stories and love. The house always seemed to be pretty full as my nana was one of seven sisters who all lived in Fleetwood. As our house was situated between their homes and the shops they all dropped in on the way to do the shopping and again on the way back, so plenty of cups of tea were dished out on a daily basis, my nana always said that was the reason she had bad knees from the constant brewing up.

As usual the pattern of my peaceful existence was about to change once more. My mum began to stay out later and later after going out drinking straight from work and when she did return the worse for wear arguments ensued. Anyway we found ourselves living with my uncle Jack and cousin Barry with my mum doing the housekeeping and generally looking after them as they both worked very long hours on the fish docks. I missed being with my nana but everything else seemed to be fine until my mum took a girl in she was fifteen and had a rough trot at life so far. She had been brought up in a care home in Liverpool because her mum (a family friend) didn't want her at least until she left school and was able to work for a living. She was placed in a job at The Norbreck Hotel in Blackpool, living in of course her mum didn't want her life disrupted with a teenager. Unfortunately not long after she started work there was a fire and she was trapped in her room and had to be rescued, luckily she only had slight burns but was traumatized and wanted to go home, her mother didn't think that was a good idea so my mum took her in. To say I was jealous would be an understatement I hated her with a vengeance. My mum seemed to have a lot more time for her than she did for me, what I in didn't realise at the time was my mum wasn't very maternal but she could cope much better with a teenager who in her eyes was nearly a human being, anyway she was called Jean and I was stuck with her. My dad turned up again around that time and talked my mum into going back with him. This time we went to Cleethorpes for a short while then to Grimsby which involved another two schools. In an amazingly short time Jean met and fell in love with one of dads crew members Pier unfortunately at a very preconscious eight so did I. They got married so as far as I was concerned I had mum back.

We then went to Denmark I don't really know if the intention was to live there or if it was an extended holiday, as I'd never had a holiday it was hard to judge.

We went over on a butter boat and I loved every minute, I was spoiled rotten by the crew as I was the only child on the boat, my mum spent the whole time in the cabin being very seasick, my dad hadn't a clue what to do with me so I was left very to my own devices.

When we got to Esbjerg, I met my Danish gran at long last and yes she did have enormous ears it's no wonder my dad checked mine. She couldn't speak any English but I was smitten and glued to her side when in the house and became addicted to the very black coffee that she used to drink in great quantities. I also had an Auntie Toova and two cousins younger than me Hanna and Anna. No male members, my dad's brothers Finn and Gunna had both drowned at very young age's whilst at sea, Finn was actually washed overboard when on the way to see me as a new born, and obviously I knew nothing of this at the time. It was a very confusing but exciting time lots of different relatives popping up, some of the older children taught me to ice skate they used to carry clip on blades so as soon as a bit of ice was spotted they would pop them on to their shoes and away they went. I got into this in a big way and managed to get in trouble because of it. I spotted a nice big icy patch did what they had done so often and found myself up to my neck in icy water, I was very unceremoniously hiked out of the water with a big pole with a spike on the end and found myself on a huge yacht. My parents were sent for, by the time they arrived I'd been dried and wrapped in a big fluffy towel. I didn't know it at the time but the chap who rescued me was none other than the king of Denmark, my mum was very impressed but their royalty are a lot more free and easy than ours, apparently he was often to be seen riding a bike! The icy patch I found was the dry dock and the yacht was there for painting.

I think we were in Denmark for about six weeks, so either an extended holiday or they fell out again, anyway back to Grimsby and yet another school. For a short while everything was ok possibly due to the fact that my dad was at sea for most of the time, the couple of days he was home were usually quite volatile. I was sat at the table eating a bowl of stew one day and he crashed his fist down so hard that my dish flew into the air and landed all over me, I think that was the straw that broke the camel's back, a huge row ensued and off we went again this time a little more dramatic as we had to spend the night in the police station under protection till they could take us in to the house to get our things the next morning. Then back on a train to Fleetwood once again, good old nana relented and took us in for my sake. I remember a peaceful couple of years; enjoyed going back to my old primary school spent all of my free time swimming. In the summer it was lovely we had a wonderful outdoor pool and I used to be there from when it opened till when it closed, I was in my element.

Of course the crunch had to come again my mum blotted her copybook once too often and we were chucked out again. We went to live with a woman called Grace, talk about being misnamed she turned out to be a bitch, there was her daughter Ann about eighteen months younger than me and Graces husband Ted.

That was the start of three years or so of hell, when Ted was at sea there were drunken parties every day, fishermen old and young staggering about the house some of them trying to cop a quick feel when the opportunity arose. I had somehow managed to get in the top stream of my secondary school and found myself with heaps of homework in order to study for my GCE exam, it was very difficult finding a quiet moment or space to do any of this. In the morning we were expected to get up and clean the living room and kitchen before going to school, we used to take it in turn. The living room involved cleaning out the fire and setting it ready for lighting, taking all the bottles glasses and overflowing ashtrays out, hoovering and polishing. Kitchen duty was much the same only instead of the fire you had to wash a very big tiled floor woe betide you if it wasn't done right, though we didn't get Grace's anger till we came home from school and by then she was well and truly drunk and cracked whichever one of us she saw first. I had the lion's share of the punishment, as Ann was such a timid little thing I used to try and take the blame for any real or imagined misdeeds.

During that period I quite often found my mum staggering about outside thinking she was perfectly sober I was embarrassed if anyone from my school was with me but more worried about my nana hearing about it so used to try and get her indoors as quickly as possible.

At that time there was a scheme launched at school that allowed a couple of students from each school in a certain area to go to a boarding school for a term, the headmistress asked my mum if she would be interested seeing as she was a single parent, so she allowed me to go, I was highly delighted to be away from that house and Grace for three months. It wasn't very far away, between Chorley and Clitheroe, as far as I was concerned it was like being on another planet, no drunks, no fights, no bashings and slapping pure heaven. I loved it so much when the next opportunity arose for another term I forged my mum's signature and convinced her she'd done it when she was drunk and of I went for another very happy three months.

Of course all good things must end so home I went for more of the same. Lots of awful things too numerous to mention without boring whoever may read this to death, I'll just put a couple of incidents in to give you a flavour. One night little Ann and I were in bed every one else was out, I could hear someone moving about the house stealthily so knew it was neither of our mums, heard a funny little clanking sound with every movement and felt it getting nearer by the second, I kept very still and prayed Ann didn't choose that moment to wake up. The door opened cautiously and through my lashes I could see the person peering round the door, I recognised him it was one of Graces many disgruntled lovers obviously looking for her, he didn't linger much to my relief but I didn't know if he had gone or not so didn't move till my mum and Grace came in a couple of hours later. When I ran down stairs to tell them we discovered our litter of six kittens had been strangled and spread around the living room, it was horrible I think it's the only time I ever saw Grace cry as she loved her cats much more than people so he had his revenge. The clanking sound I heard was his pipe banging against his tobacco tin in his pocket. Another thing that happened started as a bit of an adventure, Grace needed to go to Hull for some reason and a bloke that she strung along every now and then said his friend had a van and we could all go and make a weekend of it. When we arrived we were deposited at an old ladies house whilst the adults went to the pub, we were given mugs of cocoa by the old lady but couldn't drink it, as it was so old it had weevils in it. When we woke up the next morning it was to discover that the two chaps had dumped us all and we had no money to get back home, they had to ring up the pub they used most and ask the landlord if he'd telegraph the money for our fare home, When we got home the house had been burgled, didn't take the brain of Britain to work out who had done the deed. The two cats had been fed as well as the dog, a breakfast had been cooked and the tea made by putting the milk and sugar in the teapot. They had taken every scrap of "uncle" Ted's clothes even his socks and underwear, mum and Graces beaver lamb coats probably to carry the swag in and our radiogram, which had a drop down front so the records had kept falling out and the local headlines were 'Police follow trail of broken records'. Ann and I thought it was great all this excitement and of course they had to stay sober while all the investigating was going on. When they were dusting for finger prints (which was a joke as half the male population of Fleetwood had been there at some stage) they could only find cat's paw marks on the window sill and I thought I was very clever when I said it must have been a cat burglar, got a clout round the ear for that when the police had gone. They did catch them eventually and when the magistrate asked them if they were scared of the dog one of them said' no I just patted it on the head and it showed me round', at least he didn't let on that he knew us and did it out of spite. When Uncle Ted was in from sea there were always fights when he'd been drinking whisky he turned really vicious otherwise he was quite nice. We used to try and make ourselves invisible so as not to be in the firing line, one particular episode that stays clear in my mind was when he hurled a double wardrobe down the stairs at her but of course it got wedged, he couldn't get down and I don't suppose for one minute she wanted to get up, trouble was Ann and I had chosen the bedroom as our hiding place, she was whimpering thinking he may start on us if he couldn't get anyone else, I had a pint glass of water with me and I went and threw it in his face in the hope I would shock him out of his rage but I was so worked up I carried it through by smashing the glass to smithereens over his head I fled back to the bedroom as soon as I'd done it thinking he would kill me for sure but instead it had the opposite effect and he ended up laughing and calmed down anyway Phew! To be fair for all the other horrible stuff that occurred he never once raised his hand to us kids, just our mums.

When I was fourteen I worked on the pier in the school holidays kept me out of the way for twelve hours every day and I enjoyed it. That's when I met Tex who was to be my first proper boyfriend he was eighteen and had been to approved school and borstal so I suppose I felt a bit like a gangster's moll at first, I was very dazzled by him. Hmm, the dazzle didn't last long, I'd gone to his mum's house in Thornton about five miles away to be there when he got in from work and have tea with him and his family. When he came in he went in the back kitchen to have a wash and gestured me to come with him, like a fool I did. His job at that time was working on a local pig farm so he wasn't smelling very pleasant, anyway I was sat on the kitchen table chatting away whilst he had a wash, next thing I knew I was flat on my back on the table with the echo margarine on one side and a bottle of sauce on the other being deflowered, only there was nothing flowery about it I was horrified but didn't shout as his mother, brother and sister were in the other room and I couldn't have stood the shame. You kind of dream of the first time being romantic or at least loving that was nothing like my girlish expectations. I tried to finish with him but he said he'd tell my mum what I'd done and I was stupid enough to go along with that. It was about two months before I got rid of him and that was only because I met a nice gentle chap who actually knew Tex from school and said he was nothing but a bully and if I ignored him he'd go away and he did.

Fred was everything Tex was not, kind, gentle with a loving family. He was a trainee chef at the North Euston hotel, the biggest hotel in the town so he seemed to have prospects, not that I was thinking that far ahead it was just a step up from a pig farmer. I left school at fifteen telling my mum that I'd failed my mock GCE exam and my headmistress Miss Black who was aptly named that my mum needed me at home, luckily she didn't follow it up as with all that had been going on in my life I was no longer top of the class. The reason I wanted to leave school was because all my friends were going to work in Mullards valve factory and I wanted to go too. It was a waste of time as my mum decided to get all maternal and no daughter of hers was going to work in a factory! So I was allowed to do what I wanted for the summer as if I had still been at school it would have been my holidays but after that I would have to get a job and pay board and lodgings. I chose to work on the pier for the summer and spent all my wages on presents for my mum and nana, I used to get half a crown an hour so when I started my proper job at Stead and Simpson's shoe shop I came down to earth with a bang at the paltry £2-13and sixpence a week wages I had to tip up £2-10 shillings to my mum. Not long after I started work Fred went down on one knee and proposed to me, I said yes because I felt stupid but did rather like the ring he was proffering. When my job at the shoe shop ceased after the Christmas rush he said why didn't I get a job at the hotel so I did as a trainee waitress, just slightly more money and the possibility of tips. I decided to live in as a way of getting away from that terrible household. As it turned out we wouldn't have been there much longer as the rent hadn't been paid and the bailiffs came, I dearly wished that had happened years ago. My mum got away from Grace and the terrible influence she was.

Mum found a little bed-sitter with a kitchen and was a lot happier. I thought my life was improving until Fred started laying down the law about what we were going to do with our lives, he said I should work in all aspects of catering until I was twenty one which at fifteen seemed a lifetime away he would go to sea as a ships cook to save up for this period then we could go into hotel management! Quite a big list for a youngster but I thought at least he's ambitious. Then I met his older brother George who lived in Kendal and the list of things we were supposed to be doing were a carbon copy of what his plans had been! They didn't come to fruition either as he was a bus conductor, not that there's anything wrong with that, it was his wife stuck at home with six kids that put me off. Anyway I wasn't enthralled with my situation and I called of the engagement, he promptly went to my nana and cried at her knee, She felt sorry for him and talked me into having him back, I did and he promptly dumped me.

My next romantic episode was with a very nice chap called David, I was now sixteen and sharing my mums little bed sitter, he was thirty-two and still living at home though he had a very good job as a master scaffolder, which meant he worked away and came home at weekends. He had also presented me with a lovely shiny engagement ring (I had returned the last one). Our problems arose when he started spending all his spare time with his mates and only fitting me in when he was feeling randy, I put up with it for so long then marched into the pub and threw his engagement ring back at him. What was quite funny was in the morning he knocked on our door and came in to apologise proffering a dozen hot meat pies from our local baker I couldn't stop laughing not even a bunch of flowers. Anyway that all came to an end very amicably and I moved on. Not very far I must say as I ended up going out with Derek who had been one of his mates though I didn't know it at the time. Again he was older than me at twenty-eight but a real barrel of fun, attentive, romantic very caring. Trouble was I wasn't very interested in the sexual side of things and he cared enough to notice. He had been through a bad marriage that ended when his wife ran of with his baby to live with another guy. He naturally didn't want to get in a wrong situation and he told me to go off into the big wide world and find out if it was really him I wanted! To say I was miffed would be an understatement as I thought he was wonderful so couldn't understand it, he as it turned out knew a lot more about me than I did.

In the meantime I'd exhausted the job opportunities in Fleetwood most of which were seasonal, I even managed to work at the dreaded Mullards but it turned out I was no good at putting fiddly little valves together and they had to let me go before my training was finished, so in less than two years I'd had seven jobs not to mention three fiancés! I was also quite in awe of my youth employment officer so I marched in as if I knew what I was doing and said I'd like to join the forces, it was painless she sent me off with pamphlets for the army, navy and air force. When I read them I wasn't old enough for the navy but nearly old enough for the other two so I dip dip dipped and it landed on the army. I woke my mum up and told her she had to come with me as I was joining up and needed her permission.

Life In The Army

We had to go to the recruitment office in Preston, which was an adventure in itself as it was a train ride away. Everything was managed in the same afternoon form filling, three written exams and a medical. They asked what I thought I'd like to do as my career and I told them I wanted to become a driver. They in turn said I was much too intelligent for that and should join the signals, I had 99% in the exams so I was suitably impressed with myself and agreed to go into the signals .Had then to go home and wait for a few weeks then they sent for me to take the oath of allegiance and give me my posting dates. When I arrived all excited the wind was taken out of my sales as they sent for me on the ninth of May and I wouldn't be seventeen till the next day, to solve it they had to phone war office and they were given permission to go ahead, for twenty four hours I had the honour of being the youngest member of the WRAC. When I was sent for my basic training it was to Lingfield as the usual base Guilford was being done up.

We were issued with all our kit and shown to our quarters that would be home for the next five weeks. A corporal showed us how to put our kit away in our green tin wardrobes left us to it saying we could go to the NAAFI when we had finished. We were all a little apprehensive and for quite a few it was the first time away from home on their own, I wasn't worried as I'd had my earlier jaunts to boarding school this just felt like a more grown up version. When we walked into the NAAFI the juke box was on and playing "Somebody loves you" two girls were dancing together very closely and it was a very revealing moment for me, I just thought how lovely they looked whilst the other girls were sniggering and digging each other with their elbows. I knew without a shadow of a doubt that I was gay only in my day they called it bent.

Everything fell into place why I'd been so unresponsive with my boyfriends even though I liked them as friends, Derek had obviously seen it in me as he was a man of the world had been in the forces himself and he had been unselfish enough to let me go and find my own way. I didn't dwell on my newfound self-awareness, as we were much too busy being knocked into shape ready for our passing out parade. Everything went as it should and we were eventually allocated our camps for our various trades it was quite amusing as when we'd all talked about our choice of trade ninety percent of us had been told we were too intelligent for whatever career had been desired, they were obviously getting a bit short of signals staff, so much for me getting big headed about my exams.

My trade training was to be at Catterick after having a week at home. It passed very rapidly and I made a few friends on the way two of whom I was quite sure were bent like me but you didn't dare say anything in case they wasn't. After three months I was posted to Gloucester, Robinswood barracks and really began my time in the army. We had much nicer accommodation there, bungalow type buildings separated into rooms for three or four girls, they never had rooms for just two girls in case anything untoward transpired. When they found out I was a good swimmer I was in my element I spent most of my time training in the gym or local swimming pool, didn't have to go to work and was back and forward between Aldershot and Salisbury Swimming for Southern command. I fell for one of the girls I roomed with knew she was bent as she had a girlfriend who was a corporal so they didn't get to go out anywhere together as you weren't supposed to fraternise with other ranks. Of course I was highly delighted as it meant we could go for nights out together. Neither of us acknowledged the fact that we liked each other (like that) but on the way home when we'd had a few drinks we used to hold hands and have a kiss and a cuddle, the next morning we both pretended we'd had so much to drink we couldn't even remember coming home! All quite innocent really when I look back and think about what transpired much later. There was no likelihood of things going any further as I was clueless about what to do anyway and it wasn't as if you could ask somebody. Eventually I decided I wanted to share my knowledge about my newfound sexuality with my mum. I asked Lin if she would come home on a weekend leave with me and pretend to be my girlfriend, I thought there may be safety in numbers and said if my mum threw me out it was a seaside town we could easily book in for bed and breakfast somewhere and still enjoy the weekend. When we got to the bed-sitter instead of going in with my key I knocked on the door, easier to escape if things went wrong I thought. So when my mum opened the door with a puzzled look on her face I said " before I come in I have something to tell you I'm BENT" then stood there expecting a crack round the ear or something similar you could have knocked me down with a feather when she asked if I was butch or fem? I don't even think I'd thought it through enough to put myself in a category but given I had a shirt and trousers on and Lin was wearing a skirt and blouse I stuttered out that I was butch, shake hands with another was her reply, talk about gob smacked neither Lin or myself had a reply to that. Before we knew it we were whisked in given our tea and taken for a night out down the pub at closing time my mum said see you in the morning I'm going to stop with my girlfriend so you can have the place to yourselves. Again we were astounded and given we weren't really together spent an uncomfortable night balancing on opposite sides of the bed. We did get over the shock and ended up having a very nice weekend, my mum was the most relaxed I'd ever seen her.

In the meantime my army life was passing quite favourably made lots of new friends both men and women. Did get into bits of harmless mischief, I think it was the first time I'd been able to truly act my age and it was liberating. I didn't go any further in the girlfriend department I was too nervous having heard of the dreaded SIB (special investigation bureaux) who could come and search through your belongings, letters etc. at will. Not that there would have been anything worth finding at the time as I was still quite virginal as far as girls were concerned.

Somehow we seemed to go through our wages pretty rapidly so usually skint two days after pay day, one of the things we used to do to amuse ourselves was go to Bon-Marche and spend a few hours trying on wedding dresses, it must have really irritated the sales assistants when I think about it now.

There was a girl in our bungalow that everyone seemed to be having a moan about, I never liked bullying and decided to take her under my wing I thought maybe no one liked her because she had an unfortunate disposition. Anyway we arranged that she moved into my room when a place became available due to someone being posted elsewhere. It wasn't long before little things started to go missing, a couple of cigarettes out of an open packet, a few coins from change left on the side. The weirdest thing was missing knickers! Who on earth would want someone else's knickers? We had a communal drying room for our washing so I started to keep watch to see if any of our knickers put in an appearance they didn't of course but what I did notice is this girl never actually put any knickers out with the rest of her washing. So of we trotted to the long suffering Bon-Marche store and bought three pairs of very recognisable knickers. I left them in my draw and sure enough they disappeared after a few days. We waited till she was out then gathered round as many witnesses as possible and broke into her locker, out tumbled loads and loads of dirty knickers the ones we'd put as bait included. So we waited for her to come back and confronted her with it as soon as she did. If she'd have confessed it would have been fine but she stood there swore blind she'd never touched anything, I snapped and went for her like a woman demented, she went down like a sack of spuds I didn't hear it as I was so angry but everyone else had heard a loud crack. When they eventually dragged me off her she was in a huddle crying and holding her arm, I was even more annoyed that she'd made me behave the way I did. The outcome was we were both up on charges me for breaking her arm and assaulting her, she was charged with stealing. When the situation was explained to the Commanding officer she chose to Let me off lightly with just a couple of days jankers and a severe telling of about not taking the law into my own hands, Christine was never to be seen again so we didn't know if she'd been posted to another camp or kicked out altogether. After that I became known as Rocky not the Rocky film star too early for that but none other than Rocky Marciano the champion boxer. It was a hard name to live up to especially when on one occasion I hadn't managed to get out of games because of swimming they made me play hockey, a game I'd never played in my life, I was put in some position near the goal not doing very much when all of a sudden they came thundering down the field in my direction not looking anything like the nice young women most of them were, I dropped my hockey stick and ran for it in the opposite direction not very Rocky like at all!

My army life continued in quite an uneventful manner, plenty of long weekends leave depending on where and when I was swimming. One of my weekends happened to fall on my eighteenth birthday so my mum arranged a party at the club she used "The Blue Flamingo", sounds exotic but it wasn't. She had a cake made for me and decided to decorate it with little toy soldiers instead of candles. She did this at the club and the owner my mums friend said she would put them on. All of a sudden she exclaimed " there's only 18 soldiers!" my mum said "well that's how old she is" she was most put out as she'd been serving me for about three years and thought it was my twenty first they were getting ready for. Anyway a good night was had by all and she forgave us for pulling the wool over her eye's, then again no-one had ever asked if I was old enough just assumed if I was with my mum I must be. Yet I always had trouble getting in the cinema to see an X rated film, as I really did look very young.

The next bit of excitement was being given a posting to Malta; it came as a bit of a surprise as I'd put Singapore, Hong Kong or Germany as my preferences. Still it was take it or chance not getting offered another abroad posting. I was supposed to travel with another couple of girls but the night before we were due to go was out putting some rubbish in the bins near the guardroom and looked up to see the male orderly officer coming towards me, rather than get caught outside in my pyjamas I made a dash for the door just as one of the girls was pushing it to as there was a draft, I tried to swerve but my left arm went right through one of the panes of glass. The upshot was I had twenty-seven stitches in my elbow and wrist the girl on the other side had six in her forearm and my posting was delayed for three weeks. Because of all that I found myself going on an aircraft for the first time in my life without a friendly face with me, I'd been told to travel in civvies which was unusual, but it turned out it was a flight of mainly officers so I suppose they didn't want a lowly private sticking out like a sore thumb. A chap sat next to me and as we got in the air and food was being brought round he asked me if I would like a drink so a very tense me said yes please, when it came I was so nervous I threw it down my neck in one big gulp, the problem was it was a gin and tonic neither of which I liked with that and the combination of nerves it flew right back the minute it hit my stomach and there was nowhere to turn so my companion got the benefit of the lot, don't think he was very impressed I was too busy feeling ill to be bothered. It didn't help that we had to land at Nice to refuel when we'd only been in the air for half an hour. We were all allowed to troop off to the café in the airport all I wanted to do was find a toilet and freshen up, whilst I was in there I heard an announcement but it was in French I assume they must have said the English version as I flushed the chain. When I came out and looked through the window it was to see all my fellow passengers walking across the tarmac to the plane part of me wanted them to go without me as I wasn't looking forward to the ordeal of taking off again but common sense kicked in and I ran across to catch up. The rest of the journey I was sat alone (can't think why?) I had been told I was going to the land of "Sunshine and History", huh as I got off the plane it started to rain and didn't stop for three weeks I spent the time in wellingtons and a mack instead of my nice new uniform.

Reality kicked in well and truly when it dawned on me I would now have to do some of the work I'd been trained for yet never hardly put into practice. We had a civilian in charge of the watch I was on and luckily he seemed to take a shine to me so I didn't get told off too many for mistakes and picked it all up pretty quickly once my memory had a good jog. He kept saying something to me every time he passed me that sounded something like zarzac bera, when I asked someone they started laughing and said it means (large mammary glands) in other words he was calling me Big tits. We were told we weren't allowed to go down the GUT or Straight Street as it was called, as that was where all the prostitutes frequented. Of course that's one of the first places I wanted to go and see for myself, the other place was Selima Bay where all the lads from the army and the navy went to have fun, sounded to me like it was the best place to be and given that most of my friends were blokes that's where we headed to. We could hire a car for £1 a day so eight of us used to chip in half a crown each and though it was a bit of a squash we used to be able to go places and have fun. When I wasn't racketing around in places I shouldn't be I was of course swimming which was my joy. Again it was usually the lads I was with, one particular day I went with Ted, Terry and Fred to Golden Bay, it was a beautiful day the sea was like a millpond not hardly a ripple. We had to walk quite a long way out just to get the water as high as our waists, we had a bit of a swim and all of a sudden it started to get a bit choppy, well ,being the teenagers we were we had a great time cavorting about in it,

Then all of a sudden it started to get higher and stronger Ted said we'd better get back to shore and we all set off, or so I thought Ted was a big lad and a very strong swimmer so he reached the beach when I was halfway there, I looked behind me and Fred and Terry looked like they were playing and hadn't moved an inch I realised they were in trouble but couldn't have helped going back on my own so I got to shore sent Ted back and raised the alarm with some holidaymakers on the beach. On my way back I passed Ted who was saving Terry, when I got to Fred he was in full panic mode I tried to reassure him but was pretty frightened myself I had hold of him but every time I got back far enough to put my feet on the ledge we were washed back of it again I tried to get him to tread water and went back to get a life line, I'll never forget that, Ted and I swam out on the front and every one the beach had stepped into the shallows with a hold on the line ready to pull us all back unfortunately we couldn't see or find Fred and the only people they pulled back was us. Minutes later a helicopter arrived and they were circling the area then they dropped a rope ladder down and a man went down to the end, we saw him reach into the water an get hold of Fred's arm I thought it was going to be alright but the next thing the suction was pulling the man and the helicopter down it was awful he had to let go. They didn't retrieve his body for three weeks, his mum and dad came over and we had a memorial service, as we didn't know if he was ever going to be found. I felt guilty as if it was my fault he wasn't saved, his mum comforted me and it should have been the other way round, his poor dad never spoke once as he just couldn't stop weeping I know how he felt. When they did find him and we had a military funeral I was so overcome with grief I nearly fell in the grave. I still can't hear the last post without feeling sad and coming out in goose bumps.

After that I went off the rails, I wasn't coping very well and apart from swimming which I didn't feel I'd ever want to do again the alternative I turned to was drinking. One night I was so drunk that I got into the water at Selima bay with the thought of swimming home some of my mates dragged me out as they thought I was trying to commit suicide. I ended up in the hospital under suicide watch, I wasn't suicidal but definitely on the verge of a breakdown mainly because of the waiting, before they found Fred I had terrible nightmares of being crushed by a huge white bloated body with no head on. That stayed with me for many years afterwards. All I wanted to do was go home away from the scene off such sadness. Of course they had to have an inquest and that was awful as it was in Maltese then translated to English it was an ordeal. Once that was over they must have decided it was easier to post me back home than try and keep me on the rails there so that was what they did.

I was sent home for three weeks disembarkation leave after spending a couple of days at Guildford they gave me a warrant to go home and a return one to Chester, which was to be my new posting. In the meantime whilst I was abroad my mum had moved to a bigger place, a huge living room/come bedroom and a massive kitchen/diner a vast improvement on the last place. She was still drinking a lot but not getting into the state she did when we lived at Graces. One funny thing happened whilst I was on leave, I had made friends with a welsh girl the couple of days I was on camp I can't remember giving her my home address but she must have got it from somewhere anyway she turned up on our doorstep saying she had managed to get a weekend pass and thought she would look me up. Well we could hardly turn her away so we let her stay It was obvious she had a crush on me but I wasn't in the least interested in her. We went to the pub one afternoon and my cousin John was there and had just received a huge compensation pay out so was celebrating (he had lost his arm in a winch when he was a sixteen year old fisherman, he was now twenty one so it was worth celebrating after all that wait). After closing time we continued the party over at his house, you can imagine our surprise when there was a knock on the door and standing there was a police officer and a military police officer and her parents. Apparently the welsh girl wasn't on leave she'd done a runner but she must have told someone where she was going and why, which was more than I knew but I was being accused of luring her away. At least she told the truth when confronted and they took her away so we got back on with enjoying the party. I never heard from her again thank goodness.

So off I trotted to Chester when my leave was up it was called Saighton barracks, I was put to work on a switchboard that was in a castle on the river Dee, lovely place but again I had no clue how to work the board and spent most of my time cutting people off which didn't go down too well. Then one of the people making a call that I had messed up was having a word with me about it I was yes sir no sir I'm very sorry sir then I found out sir was a ma'am, oops. There was no hiding place as I was the only military on the board so no one else would have been saying sir or ma'am! I was doing my best to settle down but was still very distressed about Fred when I suddenly out of the blue I was sent a very important looking package, it was a Royal Humanity Award sponsored by HM the Queen. I was shocked as I had no inkling about it. At about the same time the story of it all was in the national press I don't know to this day how they got hold of the story as it was quite a while after the event. I was so upset about it all that I ran away, I didn't go home to Fleetwood as I knew that would be the first place they would look for me so hitch hiked it to London to my cousin Alex who lived in Earls court with his boyfriend (yes it did seem a bit like it runs in the family but it's a very large extended family)! Where he lived was apparently not far from a military police place and he seemed to think there would be pictures of me (a bit like wanted posters in the wild west) so he dyed my hair! It was supposed to be blonde when it was done but what he didn't know and I hadn't thought to tell him was I already had a black dye on supposedly to make me look older in my view, as most of our family had jet black hair he didn't think to ask me if it was dyed. It was 1965 I think I may have been a punk before they existed, my hair was green, orange, a kind of bluey colour and white blonde at the roots, as well as that the peroxide had dried it out and made it quite frizzy I looked like I'd had my finger in an electric socket, I went to bed fearful that it would have all dropped out in the morning. That was the least of my worries I woke up to my mums face looming over me saying "What the fuck have you done", she had a point it looked even worse in the cold light of day. She sent me off to the barbers to get it sorted, it was quite hilarious, Paddy a very boyish looking butch came with me and she had lent me her sheepskin jacket to wear which was manly in its own right, we ended up sharing it for years afterwards. Well we went to barbers rather than hairdressers, as that's what mum had told us to do, the barber was a little roly-poly very camp old queen! He lisped at us " I don't know why you boys don't come to a professional in the first place instead of ruining your lovely hair" then gave me the nearest thing to a shaved head possible all I had was a little bit of blonde bum fluff, my head looked like a very tiny Belisha beacon. It was comical though as I was trying my best to talk in a very deep voice as well as insisting that I keep my coat on which was covering my more than ample boobs. So I went from a punk to a skinhead in one day, I don't think we had them yet, just people who couldn't help being bald.

The time we spent in London at Alex and Brian's we made friends with quite a few of the gay girls he knew at the time and I was quite fascinated with the way they were so open about it, it was taboo in the army so it didn't get mentioned and my mum coming from a small town with loads of relatives had kept everything secret which was a big part of how she ended up being a drunk. I also found out that it was my mum that had talked Alex into moving away as she knew he was gay and he tried to commit suicide a couple of times so she told him the only way he'd have a life was to get away from our home town so he did. After about a week we thought it may be safe to head back home, we hadn't any money so would have to hitch hike, Paddy and her young sister decided they would come with us, its bad enough one person trying to get a lift but four seemed impossible. We went to a place not far from the motorway and started walking along with our thumbs stuck out, a big black beautiful Rolls Royce glided by us and we were making a few gestures as you can imagine never dreaming it would stop, it did much to our surprise. It was brand-new the lady who was lovely had just picked it up and she belonged to the TOC H society, which my mum said, was a Christian run thing. We hardly dared breathe in case we spoilt it. She took us to a motorway service station near the junction of the M6 and blow me down nearly straight away we got a lift in a Bentley. He explained he was a sales rep and would have to do a little detour round the potteries, which was fine by us. I was in the front with him and my mum said "my Andy is in the army" "Oh good" he said, "You must be good at map reading son" and thrust a map at me! Well after much twisting and turning my mum leaned over my shoulder and said, "It would probably help if you had it the right way up". We sorted it out eventually after much giggling and he dropped us off near Preston where we finished our journey in much less style in an ICI tanker each. We considered ourselves really lucky with the speed we got home and the lifts we had. When we arrived at the house the landlady who had the flat at the front told us the police had been around a few times looking for me and thought they didn't believe her when she said my mum wasn't there. What happened in the next couple of weeks was quite funny, a few of the girls we'd met in London decided to follow us down and move to Fleetwood for a while. There was Paddy and Maria, Jill and Rusty, Kerry and Cass, they all managed to get a bed-sitter for each couple in our house. I thought it was great, to have so many people around in my age group who were gay, not that I found out anything more about how to go on in a relationship with another woman, I expect they all thought I knew and it wasn't exactly something you could ask about especially not in the sixties. Well we had quite a few visits from the police at various times of the day trying to catch us out, the landlady was lovely she would give us an early warning and I would nip down and hide in the cellar amongst a load of old furniture. My mum could have won an Oscar with her performance of a worried mother she even managed tears, she would have given Bette Davis a run for her money. A couple of times they took away different girls from our mates thinking it may be me, they thought it was a blast as most of them were ex forces so knew the procedure. One time we were coming home from the pub in the afternoon and the police were standing on our front doorstep they come towards us and my mum said "see you later in the pub Andy", they didn't hardly look at me as they thought I was a boy with my skinhead haircut and my newly acquired men's clothes which we had bought from the pawn shop (didn't have charity shops in those days). One of the girls who didn't look anything like me, Rusty the name sort of gives it away was taken off a coach heading out of town to see if it was me. By then it was getting towards twenty-one days since I ran away and the girls who had been in the forces said after three weeks it becomes desertion rather than AWOL and is a whole different story as I could land up in the glasshouse (prison). So I decided to give myself up, Paddy went with me to the police station and I told them I had just arrived in the town and had heard they were looking for me so I thought I'd better come and see them. I had my ID card and my pay book with me but they didn't believe I was the person on the picture, after dragging all my mates in when they got the real thing they didn't want me! In the end they believed me and asked me if I would go back on my own if they gave me a travel warrant I said I would providing I could go and see my mum first as Paddy had told me how worried she was, they allowed that. They informed the camp what train I would be on so I could be escorted back to the barracks from the train station at Chester, all very civilised. We had a right giggle at their expense when I went back to see 'my poor worried mum'. A couple of plain clothed police where on the platform when my mum came to see me off. It probably gave them something to do as at the time Fleetwood had a very low crime rate.

Back at camp I was charged and given 21 days stoppage of pay and 21 days jankers, which meant a couple of hours extra cleaning duties, wearing my uniform all the time and having to be in by 10pm. It wasn't very difficult to do my extra duties as it seemed I'd acquired a fan club, a few of the girls thought I'd been brave to run away and were quite happy to clean the windows and scrub the floors and I was quite happy to let them do it. In the meantime I asked if I could get out of the army on medical grounds as even though I had been enjoying the fact I'd run away I was still very distressed about everything and seeing all the squaddies every day I just kept being reminded of Fred. Their attitude was stiff upper lip and all that; you'll get over it eventually. I asked if it would be possible to buy myself out but though It doesn't sound like much these days £350 may as well have been a million so that wasn't an option. One of the officers took me aside a couple of days later and said the only way I was going to get out was to make a nuisance of myself! Well it wasn't like I hadn't had any practice. About that time we were expecting a squad of guys from Fiji on the camp I don't know why only there was quite a bit of excitement about it and the stores had to get some extra-long beds as they were nearly all very tall. The first night they came was party night in the NAAFI and I didn't see why I should miss all the fun just because I was on jankers, so I went. When I came back very late and very drunk the orderly officer of the day was waiting for me, Instead of getting into the trouble I was expecting she helped me get undressed and put me to bed stroked my head and said "you poor little thing you have had a tough time", don't know if it went down in the log but nothing else was said about it. The next thing I did was run away again, I remember walking for miles before I got a lift it took me all night getting to Fleetwood When I arrived eventually I couldn't wake anyone in the house so sat in the outside toilet in the yard and woke up midmorning very stiff and cold. Everyone was amazed to see me standing at the doorstep once again. We didn't have police knocking on the door this time but about four days after we came in at the night time after being in the pub to see Jill and

Rusty having a full scale fight in the hallway, I waded in to try and stop them and was violently shoved away and as I went down backwards I cracked my head on the corner of the hall table, when I came round I saw what I thought was Jill and Rusty laying in to my mum I staggered out and went to the police station not far from where we lived, they sent someone round and the desk sergeant bathed my head as it was bleeding quite a lot, while he was doing it he bent round and had a proper look at me and said "you're the little bugger that was in here two weeks ago, how did you get on when you went back?" Like an idiot I told him about the three weeks jankers and pay stoppage and he said "how come you're here now as only two weeks have passed", well that was me rumbled. They asked me if I would go back on my own again and I refused so they threw me into a holding cell and there I had to stay till they sent an escort from the barracks to get me. When the two girls arrived it turned out they knew a couple of the girls from our house when they were in the army so we went home for a cup of tea and a reunion. Was charged again and given another week's jankers and pay stoppage, which didn't worry me in the least as the same girls did my extra jobs for me. It wasn't proving very easy to get kicked out so the next thing I did was get hold of a local newspaper and give them a story they obviously didn't think the content was shocking enough so made their own story up and published it! It was so bad that they had the whole camp on the parade ground asking who had given the story, I realised I'd gone too far and didn't dare own up to it so that was no help in my bid for freedom. I played up in a few other ways trying to be a pest but the straw that broke the camel's back was when I refused to dig the CO's office garden. As it was situated nearly opposite the guardroom and on the way to the NAAFI where if I did it myself everyone would see me plus my little band of helpers couldn't do it as whoever was on duty in the guardroom would see it wasn't me. Well the orderly corporal told the orderly sergeant and no I still wouldn't do it same result with the orderly officer who in turn got the Commanding officer who unfortunately was halfway to getting ready to go to some ball or other and was done up to the nines, the only thing missing was a tiara, still I refused so I was told off but just sent to my room. The next morning was pay parade before I could get anywhere near I was sent to the medical centre given a top to toe examination and proclaimed to be fit, then sent to the CO's office and given my discharge book, a travel warrant and four pence for a cup of tea on the train. The only person I could say goodbye to was the driver who dropped me off at the station. So there I was free at last.

Back To Civvies Street

Well what to do with this hard earned freedom, as I came out of the station I had to pass the employment exchange or dole as it was known as then, at least I didn't have to visit the dreaded youth employment officer as I was a grown up now. Talk about the cycle of life, the only job that was available at the time was on the pier where I'd worked before and after leaving school. That should have been a warning sign flashing in neon lights that nothing had changed only me. Still a job was a job and in the excitement and relief at being home it didn't bother me at the time. All the London girls were still there so we had a ball going out on the town I suppose it was a bit of a culture shock to Fleetwood as one day we saw a newspaper stand with the heading " Colony of lesbians invade the town" we were all wondering who they were and realised they meant us! Oh well fame at last, though I must say a few people here and there started to put their heads over the parapet when the realised they weren't alone in the town, so our group did seem to get bigger.

One day I was at work and someone suddenly loomed over me casting a shadow, I looked up to see my dad standing in front of me, which was a surprise to say the least. I didn't have a clue what to say to him so just gave him our address and sent him round to my mum! We didn't have phones in those days never mind mobiles so there was no way I could warn her, so I just gritted my teeth and got on with my job and hoped everything at home was ok. It was, the strange thing about my mum and dad was they were great as mates. Of course I had a better understanding now why all their arguments occurred in the bedroom and could at least have a bit of sympathy for my dad as he didn't know he'd married a lesbian and when she was putting him off in the hanky-panky department he was thinking she had a lover and that's why she didn't want him, well she probably may have done but it wouldn't have been another man! Strange as it may seem we had our tea, which funnily enough was stew, but I didn't end up wearing it this time, then the three of us set off for a night out in Blackpool. As the evening progressed I was getting more and more irritated with him as he was treating me like the little girl I was when he last saw me, you are drinking too much, smoking too much who are those men you were talking to? I'd been leading an independent life in the army for three years and though I was trying to give him some leeway I was getting seriously pissed off! On the other hand him and mum seemed to be getting on like a house on fire so at some stage in my alcohol befuddled brain I thought they may be getting back together even though my mum had "come out" perhaps security in her old age was a consideration, even though I knew for sure I was gay I was still having difficulty coming to terms with a gay mum. When we came out of the pub we went to Robertson's Oyster bar, which were everyone on the gay scene collected after the pub. Wasn't the best place for us to go with my dad in tow and of course he really didn't like my friends. By the time we got outside I think I had worked myself up into a bit of a frenzy and started to tell him in no uncertain terms I could remember everything he'd done to my mum when I was little and if he ever hurt her again he would have me to deal with and before I could stop myself I hauled a punch at him, think it must have been an upper cut as I felt my knuckles connect with his jaw and boy did it hurt. Three things happened, my mum looked horrified and scampered to the left, I panicked and ran the opposite way and when I glanced back my dad was standing stock still with a bemused look on his face. I was crying which was really annoying but it tends to happen when I lose my temper. I ran to the nearest tram stop then realised I hadn't any money for my fare but a very nice chap took pity on me as he could see I was upset and he saw that I got all the way home. As we walked towards my home I saw there was a police car outside and thought " my god he's killed her and it's my fault", nothing quite as bad as that a policeman came out of the house followed by my mum and he said "good grief is that who we're protecting him from?" What had happened was mum got home first as she'd ran and jumped into a taxi, didn't go to the flat but knocked on the landlady's door and told her what had happened, then my dad turned up next with the police telling them his money was in the house but didn't want to go on his own because I'd attacked him. He didn't trust banks and used to carry quite a lot of money with him depending where he was and before we went out he had hidden a wedge of his money in our flat, we knew nothing about it but he perhaps thought mum wouldn't let him in so got the police involved.

The next few days at work every time I looked up he was standing nearby watching me, he never approached me and it was frightening me, on the third day I complained to the management that a strange man was watching me and they had him removed.

When I got home he had been to my mum to say he was leaving the next day and had only wanted to make friends and say goodbye, so the following day I went to meet him in the local pub as it was my day off. We talked a little awkwardly but separated as friends. That was to be the last time I ever saw him.

One day I was at my nana's making a cup of tea for us, suddenly out of the blue she said "people are saying your mum is a lesbian is it true?" She didn't even know how it was pronounced she said les- bi- an, I dropped the tea towel on the floor trying to get myself together I said "a what?" she said "you know love it's one of those funny women who can't get a man so have a woman instead!" Trying furiously to keep my face straight I said "well that's silly as my mum married my dad so she must be able to get a man", that's true she said so it was never mentioned again. Round about that period my nana remarried she was sixty-one and had separated from her first husband when my mum was fourteen, we were thrilled to bits for her and he was a lovely man. Though I was quite enjoying myself in Fleetwood with the girls that had come up from London and my mum I didn't think I would be able to settle and decided to go and live in London, after hearing all the different stories from the girls I thought that was the place for me.

I went to my cousin Alex again he was in a different flat in Hammersmith, it was the ground floor garden flat and had plenty of room for me, plus I think they were pleased with the extra help with the rent. I settled in quite nicely and got a job with no trouble at all in Marks and Spencer on the men swear department. One of the best things about working there was they sold any leftover produce from the food hall every night for hardly any money so we may have been short of cash but we ate very well. I then started to embark on my new way of life full of anticipation and excitement. Couldn't wait to go out with the boys in my newfound 'Butch ness', Alex had given me a blazer and a tie of his so I thought I was the 'bee's knees'. I don't know if I expected a queue of woman lining up to meet me, alas that wasn't the case. The pubs Alex and Brian frequented were obviously gay but for boys mainly, there were three in Earl's court, The Boltons, The Colehern and The Lord Ranaleigh. Boltons was mainly boys who occasionally had mothers or sisters with them, the Colehern was all leather gear and moustaches, and only a certain type of boys went there, the Raleigh was mixed, straight and gay. None of this was going to be much use to me in my search for a first proper experience with a woman, though I must say we had some really good times and lots of partys. After a short while of all this mingling with the boys I was acting more like a little queen than a butch and there was nearly always some old guy trying to chat me up which we found hilarious especially as I never hardly had to buy a drink for myself and used to share the extra ones with the boys, we had quite a few cheap nights out. We usually had to make a bit of a rapid exit when these chaps realised I wasn't who they thought I was. One night we were in the Boltons and I suddenly ducked down and was hiding under the table, Alex wondered what on earth I was doing, I explained that one of the men that worked with me had just walked in and I didn't want him to see me in my butch clothes, he started laughing and asked me what I thought the man was doing in here? A good point so I got myself from under the table and went over to say hello, he looked a lot more panic struck than I had. We became friends, he was tall dark and extremely handsome with the most gorgeous blue eyes, most of the girls at work had been lusting after him since he arrived. Given that I wasn't exactly a femme fatal in girl's clothes more like a fellow in drag, they couldn't understand Shaun's sudden closeness with me and for the heck of it we sometimes walked in or out of work holding hands, it was hard keeping a straight face. All of a sudden the girls that I was used to hearing telling jokes and swearing now and again seemed to be acting in a very polite manner in front of me, I couldn't work out what was wrong until Shaun decided to confess. He'd told them that when he was younger he had tuberculosis and had been sent to a sanatorium run by nursing nuns and I'd been one of the nuns, it was a coincidence that we had met up here but I had told him I'd given up my calling, we couldn't stop laughing for ages fortunately I didn't work there for much longer so didn't have to keep up the pretence for too long. Eventually he went back to Ireland and married his childhood sweetheart after reassuring himself that he wasn't homosexual after all.

The parties we used to have nearly all took place after closing time at the pub, we used to have a night out and put the word about, and we usually had a good cross section of people from all walks of life. One night the party was in full swing and there was the sound of a kafuffle coming from the hallway, the door flew open and to my amazement a well-known pop star of the sixties was standing there screaming obscenities about how we had stolen her guests, (we didn't actually kidnap anyone). Alex tried to calm her down and told her she was welcome to stay if she wished, she didn't but left hurling abuse at her so called friends! In the meantime I was flabbergasted, never thought I'd see one of my idols carry on like that I also had a huge crush on her so couldn't believe she wore a wig and without it she was more butch looking than I thought I was!

All this wasn't helping me to meet any girls, the ones that turned up at the parties were usually established couples, so I was beginning to think I would grow old as the only lesbian virgin in the world. Two more gay boys lived in the front ground floor flat Jackie and Monique. One day they invited me in for coffee and introduced me to a girl called Cindy, I managed to stop myself saying I used to have a cat called Cindy and we all had a pleasant chat then I went back to my own flat, they'd said she was staying with them for a couple of days so I thought I may see her again and if I did would ask her where these elusive girls clubs where? That evening Alex and Brian went out without me as they were going to an all-boys club. So a night in with the telly was the plan. Next there was a knock on the door and Jackie asked if I would mind keeping Cindy company as they had to go somewhere, I didn't mind at all, my pulses were racing, a whole evening in with the first single gay woman I'd met in London! I was a little taken aback when she came in with her hair in rollers and a quilted dressing gown on, didn't quite fit in with the romantic notions I had charging through my brain like a herd of elephants. Anyway as the evening progressed so did we, sort of. Apart from a kiss and a cuddle I was unsure of the next step but she led me through the whole procedure and I got stuck in, thought I was doing everything right there was certainly lots of noises coming from her and I thought everything was great. When she left she said "that was very nice darling, do come and see me when you know what to do!" Talk about feeling deflated but it made me even more determined to get out and about and meet some more girls. I never realised at the time that the boys had set me up with her to try and give me my first experience!

Not too long after that who should turn up on the doorstep with her bag and baggage but my mum, she had decided she was missing all the fun so she moved in with us, we didn't have much choice really Alex could hardly tell his aunty to buzz off. It was a bit of a squeeze but we managed. One night we were in the Boltons and who should be there but Cindy, I felt uncomfortable seeing her for the first time since my put down but nevertheless was still eager to find out where the girls places were that I asked her if she was going to one after she, seemed like she might be but was obviously reluctant to have an innocent butch and her mother in tow, though I must say my mum looked more like she was my dad by this time. At closing time we decided to follow her I felt like some private eye in a cheap detective story. Neither of us was used to the underground but we managed, we didn't know what her destination was so buying a ticket was a bit dodgy; we could have probably travelled to the end of the line with the one we bought. Against all odds we managed to keep her in sight and carried on following her outside the station. Though we didn't know it we were in Soho in the west end of London, after a few twists and turns she went down an alleyway so we were peeping round the corner to see what happened next. She reached up and tapped on a hatch, paid some money and disappeared inside, we followed after a few minutes and did the same hoping against hope you didn't have to be a member, it was half a crown (2/6d) each to go in. when the door was opened it was quite dark and lots of loud music thumping out of the juke box, there were two places where it was a little lighter and we were just in time to see Cindy going into one of them. We trotted behind her and her expression was something to behold when she saw us. She stammered out that she couldn't have brought us as she had come here to work (in the cloakroom), it was a tiny little room and hardly anyone took their coats off, they would have probably been stolen. It was quite obvious she was lying, as you don't have to pay an entrance fee to go into work. Well because of her barefaced lie she had to stay in there for most of the night. The club was called the Limbo and was going to be my home from home for the next few years. They didn't sell any booze just soft drinks, tea or coffee, so we couldn't understand why everyone was so amazingly merry!

Well the next night we went to the Limbo without having to follow anyone and soon found out why everyone seemed so perky. We kept seeing a girl going in and out of the club on her return she always went back to the last person she'd spoken to and seemed to hand them something, eventually we caught her eye and called her over and said could you get some for us she said she would and they (whatever they were) would be 6d each, so we bought a pounds worth each. When she brought them back they were in strips of plastic like they used to sell aspirins in the chemist. We thought well here goes nothing and had a strip, each which was about five. Wow we were full of energy couldn't stop talking and thought it was great, Fortunately for us Jill and Rusty who stayed at our house in Fleetwood turned up, they had come back and found out where we would be from Alex. We were so overjoyed to see them (probably more enthusiastic because of the pills), it was nice to have someone we knew at the club we didn't feel like quite the outsiders we were. In the meantime we had swallowed quite a few more pills, we gave some to the girls who said they were called blueys, when we said how many we had taken they said we would have a terrible comedown and stayed with us to make sure we were ok. Well it's all a bit of a haze but we ended up at another girls flat as we didn't dare go home like we were as Alex wouldn't have approved. My memory of that is coming round in a bedroom and thinking I was in a toy shop as the walls had shelves all around the room absolutely filled with dolls. I got up and went looking for everybody else and found them in the kitchen trying to spoon feed my mum with tomato soup, saying she needed food inside her to help the pills wear off. When we left there we went to a pub and rang Alex to let him know we were alright, at this stage we had been out for three nights so thought we had better head for home, we still hadn't had this terrible "come down" that the girls expected but as we walked down Hammersmith grove I suddenly started laughing and my mum said what's so funny, she obviously couldn't share my hallucination but I could see marching towards me a squadron of upside down buckets with their handles looking like chinstraps, I knew it wasn't real but they looked so comical I couldn't stop laughing, that was the only side effect I had. Went to sleep when we got back woke up and was ready for another night out. I had missed a day at work but was back at work the next day without any bother as it was the first time I'd been off, I told them it was "something I ate!"

The next thing on the agenda was finding a place for us to live; it was a bit cramped in the flat with four of us, and what if I was to find someone I wanted to bring home? I managed to find a student bed sit in Notting Hill, Linden gardens. It was a huge room with three single beds a tiny kitchen in a cupboard a small table and chairs. We had to share the bathroom but luckily for us it was the next door down the passage. Because I'd moved I changed my job I wasn't used to having to travel to work and London was so vast everything seemed such a long way. So I managed to get a job in Nyman's Bazaar. It had everything, beautiful china dinner services, crystal glass, pots, pans, dustbins, dusters, you name it and it could probably be found. Mr Nyman was lovely, he was a Jewish chap the father of five boys, who had longed for a girl, I became his surrogate daughter, and we had a bit of a mutual admiration society going on there. I worked hard for him and he appreciated it, good job he didn't know I was stoned out of my mind half the time I was at work. Turns out I was quite a good saleswoman, have always had the gift of the gab and of course it was enhanced by the couple of pep pills I had in the morning when I left the club to go home and get ready for work. Of course by this time I was leading a double life, stalking about the club and pubs at night time in all my men's clothes, rushing home on the first tube in the morning to change back into girls clothes, I'm exhausted just thinking about it now but of course it was the 'swinging sixties 'and things where much different then. One day a man came running in, it was a long narrow shop, he ran straight to the back and jumped on to a ledge he was closely followed by a couple of police men. He started hurling anything he could at them to try and keep them at bay of course he was tackled in the end. What had happened was he had tried to change a forged prescription at the chemist opposite for drugs, they had rumbled him and discreetly phoned the police so when he saw them he legged it into our shop which unfortunately for him had no back door. The newspaper headline was ' A bull in a china shop'; luckily for us he had landed up where it was mainly pans and cutlery so not much china was damaged. Looking back I don't know how I managed without wrecking the place, I had very rarely been to bed was usually keeping going with a couple of pills, yet I was up and down ladders to really high shelves all the time keeping them dust free as well as serving them if required, I only had one mishap and that was in the stockroom upstairs I put my arm through some racking to switch the light on and caught one of the boxes with my elbow, it crashed to the floor, I was mortified it was a gross of very delicate liqueur glasses that were 19s-11d each, my wages at the time were about £8-10s a week, I'd have been paying forever, he came to see what was keeping me up there for so long to find me sitting on the floor surrounded by broken crystal crying my eyes out! I perked up considerably when he gave me a hug and said don't worry they are insured.

Well at long last things started to happen for me in the romance department, well more lust if I'm honest I was acting like a rampant teenage boy I suppose, so many women so little time. I was still shy about approaching anyone but found if I stood around looking available someone would inevitably approach me, which was great I'm afraid I wasn't very choosy in those days anything with a pulse would do. They weren't looking for long term relationships either I was at the time what they called "A Mystery", so any available fems were likely to steam in and give it a go so to speak, I didn't know all this at the time but I wasn't complaining, after living in a desert I was now splashing about very happily in a lagoon! All the time I was gaining experience; in the back of my mind all the time was the parting shot from Cindy, which had really rocked any confidence I had.

One night I was in the Boltons and over at the bar was this tiny little lady with the longest hair I had ever seen it was nearly down to her ankles, the odd times that it parted I glimpsed a very pretty face, she was with a couple of men one of them was gorgeous in his own right. Somehow after half a dozen drinks I got brave enough to sidle up to them and start a conversation, they were brother and Sister Ken and Moya. I was smitten, as it was nearly closing time we said our goodbyes but arranged to be in the pub the next night. I was like a dog with two tails all the next day and even better it was Friday so I didn't have to go to work the next day as the shop didn't open on Saturdays being Jewish owned and every other week I had Sunday off and this was that weekend whoopee! My mum came out with me that night a combination of moral support and nosiness. When we arrived Alex and

Brian were there as well so was a bit like a family reunion, I couldn't keep my eyes away from the door and as time was passing was getting more and more anxious that they wasn't going to come. When they did I felt a huge surge of relief and all but galloped over to them, I can't remember what they said about why they was so late, but they asked me if I'd like to go to a party so I said yes and could mum, Alex and Brian come? No just me, so I went and told them that I was going and to expect me when they saw me. There was another man and women with them don't remember her name but apparently she was a choreographer for the ballet, he was called Andy and was an actor. When we got to the flat in Chiswick and it was all in darkness I was thinking hello what happened to the party, still I was there it was an adventure so what the hell! Once inside the huge living room was covered in dustsheets as it was being decorated so that only left the kitchen and the bedroom available, I may not have been as worldly wise as a lot of people but I wasn't completely stupid either. He moved one of the covers and opened a cocktail cabinet that was crammed with every drink imaginable and asked what we wanted to drink I said vodka and was presented with the whole bottle and a glass, Moya got what she wanted grabbed my hand and dragged me off to the bedroom! Quick work or what? Turned out he was her husband not her brother and was into kinky threesomes, she wasn't as into it as much as he was and had suggested why not a girl instead of the usual man which was where I came in! I thought I'm not having any of that so I bolted (not out of there), I locked the door and we proceeded to have a fantastic night, not that I can remember half of it being in possession of a whole bottle of vodka but I know I was trying to share some of my new found prowess. Well it must have worked, I woke up in the morning to being served a sumptuous breakfast in bed, a bath run for me and lots of kisses and cuddles, fighting off my hangover I thought well this is the life. I asked how Ken had been with her and she said fine that it was him who cooked my breakfast and had himself a very nice night with the actor and the choreographer so wasn't worried about us in the least. I suppose at the time I thought this was all very sophisticated a bit like film stars. When I eventually appeared in the living room which had been cleared of dust sheets and was very nice, especially compared to our grotty little bed sit I was informed that Ken was going to the pub he had put a homemade steak and kidney pudding on for dinner and did I want anything bringing back, I asked him if he'd pick me up a packet of cigarettes and off he went. So we had the afternoon to get to know each other without being smashed out of our heads with drink, though to be honest I think it was only me that had too much. Turns out they had been married about ten years and he suddenly wanted to experiment with threesomes she said she'd give it a try but had always been curious about going with a woman so I had satisfied her curiosity and she would like it to carry on please, to say I was flattered would be an understatement but I said I would love to see her again so long as they didn't expect me to join in any hanky-panky that involved anyone else! She was a top something or other for the bank of England and he was a television producer, heady stuff for a humble shop girl to take in. When he came home he was charming towards me and presented me with a two hundred carton of fags I panicked and said I only wanted twenty but he said they were a gift. We had a lovely dinner he was a very good cook and I said I should to be making tracks home so where was the nearest tube station as I hadn't a clue where I was in relation to where I lived. He said not to worry and rang a cab firm where he had an account and gave him my details and told me if ever I needed a cab I wouldn't have to pay just tell them to put it on his account, WOW! I never took advantage of the offer except if I was invited over and had to make my own way rather than meet them in the pub. It was nice to know I could though and made me feel quite special (rather than available which with hindsight was probably what it was).

In the meantime I was still regularly frequenting the Limbo, getting to know a few more of the regulars. I didn't know it at the time but I was just about to meet the person who was going to become my lifelong friend. Not that you'd have thought so in the beginning. You know when you get a burning feeling at the back of your neck and just know someone is looking at you, well it was like that and every time I looked round all I could see was this little butch glowering at me, If you are in my age group you will remember 'Archie Andrews', who was actually a ventriloquists doll and the odd time you saw a picture of him he was wearing a navy and red striped blazer, I never really understood the ventriloquist bit as the shows had originally been on radio as we didn't have television at the time , but I do remember listening avidly. The little glowering butch was wearing the same blazer, which has always stuck in my mind, this glowering continued over a couple of nights. My mum hadn't been out for a few nights but when I told her she said why don't you just ask her? Anyway the next night we both went to the club and mum went down first as I was talking to the guy on the door, when I got to the bottom of the stairs who should she be talking to but the glowering butch, who was looking all smiley and friendly till she laid eyes on me. I said "what are you talking to her for, she's the one I've been telling you about?" My mum laughed and said "Chris she's lovely" Chris then chipped in "I don't think you should be talking to her! She's horrible", my mum retorted, "that could be a bit difficult, this is my daughter". Anyway she suggested we both go to the coffee bar round the corner and get it sorted out which we did. It turned out someone told her I had designs on a girl that she really liked, I hadn't a clue what she was talking about but with a bit of probing found out that it was the girl whose flat we'd been to when we had all our pep pills the first time, I barely remembered what she looked like let alone fancy her I just know that everyone called her "Penny Anne" we never ever found out why either. When the air was cleared we became firm friends and still are and apart from the initial glowering we have never had an argument or a cross word, she is my little big sister, and I am her big little sister as there is two years between us.

Back to my dalliance with Moya, it was all going surprisingly well I thought then out of the blue she asked if I would go and live in Spain with her if she left Ken, that took me by surprise I just thought I was having a little adventure nothing too heavy She reckoned she'd fallen for me, I was shocked. I said I would have to think about it, as it had never entered my head to live abroad. When I stayed with Moya, Ken used to take himself of somewhere for the night and leave us alone, The next time I went when I woke up and came out of the bedroom there he was brandishing an axe! I fled and he was chasing me round the flat, I managed to barricade myself into the bathroom and Moya at some stage calmed him down and I was able to creep out and go home, much later. Funnily enough I never went back there but I did speak to Moya on the phone and she had told him that she was in love with me and what her plans where, needless to say I didn't tread that path again but it had been quite exciting whilst it was happening. (Quite by accident a few years later I dialled the wrong number and Ken answered, oops, so I asked how they were getting on and he told me she had left him and they were divorced).

Having decided I was a lot more experienced I thought I would look Cindy up so found her address from Jackie it was in Earls Court. So of I trotted off one day and knocked on her door to my surprise it was opened by a young gay guy, he said she was busy and did I have an appointment? No but was sure she would see me, turns out she was a prostitute that was a surprise I knew quite a few of the regulars at the club were on the game as they used to be in and out all night between punters but I'd never met one with a flat to do it from! When she came through I said "well you told me to come and see you when I knew what I was doing, so here I am" Talk about cocky I wasn't the shy little private any more. So off we went and did the deeds and boy did I give her a work out after putting me down like she did after my first time, I showed no mercy I was probably way over the top but she shouldn't have upset me so much! When I'd finished with her I said "will that do for you", then I left feeling very satisfied that I had restored the balance in my life. After that I did occasionally see her in the pub or club and she used to try and come on to me but I wasn't interested at all.

I was in the Limbo as usual and had been in the toilet, when I came out the club was deserted except for two men standing at the counter of the coffee bar. I thought it was strange as when the police raided the club and emptied it they checked the toilets as well so I thought it couldn't be a raid, but where had everyone gone? I went up to the counter to get a coffee, the young lad who was serving was as white as a sheet I thought perhaps he wasn't feeling so good. Anyway before he served me the coffee I saw out of the corner of my eye one of the men take a pint bottle of whiskey from the inside pocket of his overcoat, I quickly changed my order to a bottle of coke and a glass which I promptly plonked down in front of the guy with the bottle of whiskey, the boy behind the bar went whiter than ever and the man gave me a quizzical look, unperturbed I wiggled the glass in front of him fully expecting to get a shot of whiskey, (it was an unwritten law in the club if anyone had booze they shared it!). He poured some in my glass and I shared my coke with him and his friend. I can't remember what we chatted about but we passed a pleasant hour and finished the bottle of whiskey between us, when they were leaving we shook hands and off they went. A few moments later everyone came streaming back into the club, my mum came hurtling over asking me if I was all right. I was more than all right feeling quite euphoric after drinking a third of a pint of whiskey! Turns out my drinking pals were quite notorious, one of the Kray twins (never did find out which one) and "Charlie the Axe"! I couldn't understand why everyone had left the club as I had found their company to be very pleasant, apparently everyone was scared they were looking for someone and there may have been trouble. Not long after that they were sent to prison, so I had a brush with the infamous without even knowing about till later.

One night there was a whole gang of my mates and myself down the Limbo and it was a very busy night, more so than usual. Every time I went to the toilet I had to excuse myself to get past a bloke that had been stood there all of the time, as I came out the last time he made some scathing remark and we started an argument, it was getting out of hand and he offered me outside, being the big tough guy I thought I was I said ok, plus all my friends were sat near the stairs so I thought they would come and help me. As I was going up the stairs I was making all the gestures of a punch up to them hoping one would notice but they didn't! Once outside in the mews a slanging match ensued but we were a few feet apart so nothing disastrous happening, there was quite a crowd gathering round, at some stage someone had gone inside the club and said you'd better get up there your daughter is in trouble. I think it may have died a death as a stupid squabble but we were stood either side of the door and as my mums head appeared he said "you can fuck of you dirty lesbian breeder!" That did it I threw a punch at him, the next thing I was picking myself up from the floor as my mum was on the way down, more people had joined in but unfortunately for us they were his friends not ours, anyway we were getting a right beating, it only stopped when someone shouted that the police were coming, every one dispersed which just left us two scraping ourselves up of the floor. At last the news had filtered down to our mates in the club and they came and gathered us up and took us round to the "Coffee Pot" in Wardour Street to get us cleaned up. Oh boy did we need it, the mews was where the hamburger stands that were dotted around the west end all day were stored and before they put them in the building they used to tip all the fat and the onion water out into the mews. We were covered in all this as well as our own blood, I had a jacket on that Ken had given me before he tried to chop my head off it was lovely the most expensive thing I had ever owned It was 30 guineas, it was only joined together at the shoulders the rest was ripped to shreds. When we got to the Coffee Pot Charlie the owner took us out and had to hose us down, we were in a right old state my front tooth had been kicked in so only a stump was left, both of us were sporting black eyes already a sign of what we would be like when the bruising had chance to come out. We had made friends with a man with the unlikely name of Bamboo Chris; we knew he was a bit of a gangster as people showed him a lot of respect and if we went out with him we never had to pay to go in any of the clubs. He lived across the road from us in Linden gardens and sometimes came across for breakfast, he thought it was great us being mum and daughter and living the same sort of life style he was of Greek origin and they really revere their mums so we thought he had sort of adopted mine. Well there was a bit of a carry on in the café, we were just on our way back in dripping from head to foot he was shouting "whose hurt my girls, whose hurt my girls". Someone had gone to the Alphabet club in china town and told him we'd been beaten up. Someone told him the guy's name was Adam West (not batman), It was just like something out of a movie they said he went that way with that he ran out of the café flagged down a taxi which happened to be an old fashioned one with a running board he jumped on it and said follow that man! It was to be the last time we saw him for three years, he caught the man and stabbed him and was sent to prison, we didn't find out for ages what had happened and when we did he didn't want us to visit at the prison so wouldn't send a visiting order.

One night a few of us were on the way to the club and we wondered why Rusty wasn't with us? Jill said she had gone for a job interview and would meet us in the club, we thought it was a strange time for a job interview especially as Rusty thought work was a dirty word! Eventually she joined us in the club and was crestfallen, the employer thought she was too young, mum wanted to know what the job was and she said it was a maid's job. So my mum said "well I'm older than you and how hard can it be?" So Rusty took her round introduced her and left her there, when my mum came back she was wetting herself laughing, she hadn't realised what sort of a (maid) was required, not to serve tea and biscuits but to let in and vet the punters to a prostitute, Rusty had failed to mention that in the job description. My mum started work the next evening from 8pm to 1am £3 an hour and a tip with every punter that crossed the threshold. On a quiet night my mum would sometimes earn more than Wendy as she got her hourly rate no matter what. She had to wear a skirt for this job and look like the respectable middle aged woman she was supposed to be just in case they had a visit from the police, one girl at a time was classed as alright but two or more made it a brothel. My mum took to it like a duck to water and often had some comical tails to relate. One particular chap used to come early in the evening wearing bowler hat, pin stripe suit and carrying a brief case. The first time my mum let him in, Wendy came out of the bedroom and said could you do me a favour I can't do this alone? Mums mind was boggling but when she told her it didn't involve having sex and what her part in it was although she felt a bit shy she said ok. What he had in his briefcase was a set of reins for a horse, it took huge self-control for my mum not to laugh as he was standing there naked except for his socks with the reins and bit on, a hand brush shoved up his backside by the handle was supposed to be his tail! Mums job was to control the reins and gallop him round the room whilst Wendy skipped about in front of him dangling a carrot just out of reach, mum soon got out of her embarrassment and was cracking the reins and shouting "giddy up there that's a good boy" with lots of fervour, when Wendy let him catch her up and have the carrot that was it as far as mum was concerned so she went back to her crossword and cup of tea in the kitchen. When he'd gone Wendy brought my mum a five pound note in, he'd said it was the best time he'd ever had, praise indeed as the punters had to pay before they went in and that always included a tip for the maid which was usually five shillings! Obviously it wasn't all plain sailing (or riding), sometimes awkward drunks turned up and it was mums job to vet them and eject them if required, wasn't always easy when confronted with a twenty stone rugby player but in extreme circumstances a threat to call the old bill usually worked. One night we were all wanting to go to the club but didn't have any money to get in with, so mum said if I came up to the flat she would be able to give us our entrance fee once she'd been there a couple of hours. When I got there she put her finger to her lips for me to be quiet and led me in, I assumed there must be someone in there doing the business but before I had chance to breath she'd opened the door and shoved me in! Wendy was standing in the middle of the room ready to greet me, my mum had said she was pretty but she was beautiful I must have stood there with my mouth open she said just a minute and went in to my mum, I heard her say " I can't do him he's much too young" my mum said "he's older than he looks but it's his first time so be gentle with him", as she reluctantly returned to the room I cracked out laughing and gave the game away. She called my mum all sorts but thought it was funny too. (We might be poor but we do see life). I can't remember how long my mum worked there but it was quite a while and we all became friends out of work time as well she always came to Alex's parties when we went.

Talking of parties, one night someone came down the club and put the word round that there was a big party going on if anyone was interested, well free booze it was a no-brainer about twelve of us went all girls when we got outside the mews there were three or four big black limo's waiting so we all piled in ready for an adventure, I haven't a clue where we went but it was a huge Victorian type house nicely decorated in one room there was a table lavishly set out with food, the room next to it had a bar with anything you would care to drink and there was music playing though no one was dancing. The other guests seemed to be mainly Chinese looking chaps, all was going along swimmingly when someone announced everything was ready in the other room! I held back a bit but had a peek in when everyone was in and thought no this isn't my cup of tea, there was a big screen and a very detailed porno movie in progress so I sidled of to another room. Which turned out to be a bedroom anyway I sat on the end of a very high bed and was swinging my legs as I sat there looking round feeling a little bored and wondering how long the dirty movies would be on for. My foot banged into a box so I looked under the bed and there were lots of cardboard boxes so I thought I'd be nosy and have a little look, blimey it was worse than the film! Hundreds of dirty pictures I was nearly standing on my head wondering how on earth they got into some of the positions, anyway I must have been carried away with my little private viewing as I could hear footsteps coming towards the room so I kicked the box back under the bed and just crammed the photos into my pocket. After a few more drinks we were all taken back to Soho and deposited back at the mews entrance, a few of the girls came back with a lot more money than they left with so it wasn't hard to guess what had gone on during or after the film session. What became of the dirty photos? Well we went back to Fleetwood for a week to see my nana, I was in the pub one night and told one of the lads about these photos he told me to bring them with me the next night I did and he sold them to the fishermen for a fiver each something to keep them company the three weeks they spent at sea.

First Partner

The next memorable night was when I met the girl who was to become my first proper relationship. Again it was in the good old Limbo, Chris and I were talking to a couple of girls and a little while later one of them was feeling sick so we offered to take her home as Chris had a car, she was staying in a basement flat in Kentish town. I know it's an unlikely way to meet the first love of your life, as she was about seven months pregnant and feeling very poorly with it. We got chatting and we ended up in a relationship, which again was a little strange as she wasn't well enough to go out a lot so I used to spend all my weekends at Kentish town with her. The flat was owned by a funny little old man (well he seemed old to me), who was very kind but a little bit nutty. He had been in the flat for years and in the war he worked for the railway which ran alongside where the flat was, part of his job was to help remove dead bodies off the railway lines. Apparently there were quite a few of these with the blackout no wonder he was a bit strange. Anyway Jose and I were getting on famously. She had ended up getting pregnant because of a very strict very catholic father, who on finding out she was a lesbian had more or less terrorised her into going out with a man! I know it's true I eventually met him. Basically she went with the first man she met who happened to be the window cleaner at the garage she worked at, they had an undignified fumble in the back of his van, neither enjoyed it and she didn't see him anymore. Sods law she was pregnant, that didn't please her father either and he threw her out and banished her mum from seeing her. A girl she knew took her round to the flat belonging to Ted and he took her in, it wasn't perfect but somewhere to lick her wounds. The flat only had one bedroom but it contained a double bed and a single, the double was for Jose and the single was Teds, not as bad as it sounds as he still worked on the railway and did the night shift. Bless him he didn't know the half of what went on in his home when he was at work. The girl that had taken Jose to him was a drug addict not the odd pep pills but the hard stuff, heroin and to maintain her habit she was on the game and wasn't averse to taking the odd punter to Teds whilst he was working, which wasn't a good situation for Jose to be in whilst pregnant. I tried to get her to move in with me but she said she didn't want to move till she had the baby, I suppose, though it wasn't ideal she did know them better than me.

In the meantime we were having a lovely sexual relationship I suppose when it's the first time you're in love everything seems that much better and special. The only fly in the ointment was when she tried to touch me! I kept stopping her, as that hadn't happened to me before with the others I had been with but I had heard the words "being turned over" bandied about. That was when a feminine girl had made love to the butch with her doing the touching I got the impression from other butches that was a big no, no! How stupid can you be, the only reason this came about is the role playing you had to do in those days the butches had to look boyish so as to be recognised by the feminine gay girls and they usually did the approaching rather than the other way round so no big mistakes were made, there was always an exception to the rule which I'll tell you about later. Anyway very nervously I told her I hadn't been touched that way by a woman so she said it was about time I was! Wow, talk about mind blowing especially when she started to creep down the bed to do what I'd done many times, I was embarrassed and tense but when it happened I thought I was going to die the feeling was so intense. Afterwards I said to her "is that what I do to you? How can you bear it?" She thought it was hilarious I had just had my first ever orgasm and when I got over the shock I thought it was wonderful.

A rather big event took place while we were staying at Ted's, one morning the door was nearly hammered down and when opened by one of the girls the police came swarming in on a raid, search warrants and everything. We were told to stay where we were and not move from room to room, well Jose and I were still in bed as was Lorraine a girl who didn't stay very often but had stayed the night before as Ted was at work, he hadn't actually come home yet so it must have been early. A male detective was left in the bedroom to make sure we didn't hide anything. Jose suddenly started rummaging around in her handbag ostensibly for a hanky, having done that she gave me a nudge under the covers and passed me a little package wrapped in silver paper, I remembered what it was, a couple of weeks previously another butch who liked her had turned up not knowing about me and gave her this little bit of hash, strange gift as Jose didn't even smoke normal cigarettes never mind hash. Anyway she had just dropped it in her bag and forgot all about it. There we were lying in bed with a bit of hash between us the detective standing at the end of the bed, well what else could a girl do. I ate it and had the cheek to ask the guy to pass me a bottle of tizer that was on the dressing table to wash it down, I swallowed the silver paper as well. After a lot of stamping about in the rest of the flat the senior guy came in and said right get dressed your all going to the station, he did have the decency to put a female constable in the room with us. That's when things got a little strange they took one look at how heavily pregnant Jose was and said she didn't have to go! She could have been the biggest drug dealer on the planet but they didn't take her. At the station we were given a full body search which wasn't very pleasant especially for Lorraine and I who had never been in trouble, the other girls had all been in prison before for one thing or the other. When it was my turn to be interviewed I gave all my particulars where I lived my job and all the rest he said I didn't seem the type to be mixing in this sort of company and I said I was there because that's where my girlfriend was, the one they didn't bring in! He showed me a package about the size of a bar of chocolate and asked me if I knew what it was I didn't but could have had a wild guess. Eventually they let me go saying I would have to appear in court as would all of them, as we were being shepherded out poor old Ted was being brought in and he looked petrified. By the time I got home the hash that I'd swallowed had kicked in and I thought everything was funny My mum couldn't work out why I was laughing at something so serious till I told her, good job it took a long time to affect me else they may have realised. When I talked to the other girls about this big block of hash the police showed me they swore blind they'd never seen it and I believed them because apart from myself Jose and Lorraine the other three were heroin addicts so what would they want with that, the police couldn't charge them with the stuff they did have as they were registered and it was prescription drugs they had on them. So the police had miraculously found this great chunk of hash very conveniently. When it eventually came to going to court the girls that had been in trouble before all had solicitors, as did poor old Ted who had done nothing wrong only been soft in letting what he called his "girlies" walk all over him. Lorraine's dad came with her and my mum came with me dressed in a ladylike fashion to look the part of the worried mum. I didn't feel I needed anyone as I knew I was innocent, When the charges were read out I was outraged, this one chunk of hash that they'd shown me had managed to split itself into three pieces and they alleged they found one bit in the bread bin in the kitchen, another on the mantelpiece in the living room and worst of all the other bit was supposed to have been in a little storeroom that Ted always had locked and no-one else had access to the key. He used to lock his spare food in there teabags and the like so his girls didn't eat him out of house and home. You didn't have to be a legal eagle to know he was being railroaded and it was him they were after. Because we weren't being represented we were asked if we had anything to say or any questions to ask, I did with a vengeance, how had this piece of hash morphed into three and put in the only places where the other girls where why they didn't take Jose when they raided the place and so on I actually caught them out in two or three lies, so the charges against Lorraine and I were dropped and they merrily went on to give the other girls suspended sentences and poor old Ted was given a seven year prison sentence for allowing drugs to be used in his house and also running a house of ill repute. It was laughable as he was so nutty but so innocent. I did go and see him once in Brixton prison it was so sad as there wasn't much of him in the first place and he was wasting away and still couldn't understand what he was doing there.

A New Life

By the time all that had gone to court the baby had been born so we were no longer at the flat anyway. We woke up one morning and Jose said she was bleeding a bit, I was clueless what to do about it, we had moved from Linden gardens back to Hammersmith Grove where I was in the first place, a flat had become vacant so we moved back as it was bigger, also it had a shared coin phone in the hallway so I was able to ring and get a message to my mum to come over to us. She did and said there was no need to worry it was just a bit of spotting. Later on she went into labour so we rang the hospital and they said it was too soon yet to ring up when the time shortened and the pains got worse. Of course I was like a gibbering idiot throughout this time just as bad as any expectant father. Round about teatime her waters broke and I rang the ambulance, the birth was to be at The University College Hospital. When we arrived Jose was whisked off in one direction and we were sent to a waiting room with all the other expectant fathers. They had a tannoy system in the room so they said a name and where to go, all quite sensible. They called a name out a few times and no-one went my mum suddenly said "it's you! You silly bugger", of course they were calling for Mr McNee which was Jose's surname so I wasn't tuned into it. I went to the nurse's station and they took me to a small side ward and said I could stay with her and not to worry the baby wouldn't come for at least four hours. She had been having bouts of sickness all through her pregnancy and today was no exception, the only difference was I was feeling pretty sick myself and we were fighting over who should hold the kidney bowl! She was gripping my hand and nearly breaking my fingers in the process but at a time like that you just don't care. About fifteen minutes after I went in the room she said "it's coming I can feel it coming" I said "don't be silly they said at least another four hours", with that comment she threw the covers back and said have a look, my god it was coming I could see the top of its head, talk about panic stations I rang the buzzer and didn't let go till someone came, when they did it was a full house, the midwife the doctor and three or four students as it was a training hospital. I found myself squashed back against the wall by the side of the bed and saw everything as it happened, I was fascinated but traumatised as well, I must have gone a funny colour as when the baby was out they said come on daddy we'd better let you sit down, they took me to a room across the way sat me down and started to loosen my tie, I tried to deepen my voice and said its ok I'll do that, she gave me a glass of glucose and orange and when I'd recovered enough took me back to see 'my daughter', they put her in my arms and it was love at first sight she was beautiful not all wrinkly or anything. Jose had no interest in her whatsoever it was as though she gave birth and that's it, she didn't even want to hold her all she wanted was her compact out of her bag. She had gone straight into what we now call baby blues but I didn't know that then.

When I went to see her the next day she had been put in a ward but was in a side room all on her own, when I asked her why she said it was when they discovered that she wasn't married she was put there, it was still frowned upon to be a single parent in those days so when her paperwork had caught up with her they discovered I wasn't her husband! She didn't dare tell them I was a woman, as that would have made matters even worse. So she had told them I was her boyfriend and I wanted to marry her but seeing as the baby wasn't mine she wanted to make sure that I would still want her and the baby! They seem to have accepted that because apparently the doctor wanted to talk to me about birth control to make sure it didn't happen again before we got married. I thought it was hysterical couldn't wait to get home and tell everyone. By the time I did get back my mum was standing at the door watching out for me with a case in her hand, I laughingly asked her if she was leaving home. Jose had rung from the hospital, not long after I had left the ward sister had been in and had been very scathing and unkind about her situation and she wanted to come out. So mum had borrowed a set of baby clothes from a woman in one of the flats who was pregnant and a set of clothes for Jose from another of the girls who was a similar size. My mate Chris who has always been more practical than me had put £5 to one side so we would be able to bring them home in a cab. So back we went and brought her home, we had one of the nurses running behind us saying you can't do this all to no avail because we did! When we arrived home we had to go and knock the local chemist open as we had no baby food, nappies or anything, fortunately he lived over the premises.

So a totally new way of life was about to start for me, because I'd moved back to Hammersmith of course my job had changed once again I was now working in a factory called Lemco, as were most of the girls who lived in the house. Rusty amazingly had decided to start work there because we all had but she was always being late, the manageress had taken a shine to her so bought her an alarm clock to make sure she arrived on time. Her working life didn't last long but she did have a fling with the manageress! In the meantime Jose wasn't getting on very well with motherhood at all, I had managed to inform her mother that she was a grandma to a beautiful baby whose name was to be

Wendy she was thrilled to bits and as soon as she could manage it without her husband finding out she was coming to see us. I was hoping that with some guidance from her mother Jose might come out of her depression but she didn't. It was quite strange really she seemed to be fine in all aspects of her life it was just a stumbling block when it came to the baby. It was getting a bit cramped in the flat with the baby and all it entailed so I set about finding a place for just us and did, so of we went back to Notting Hill, this time it was Clanricarde Gardens, we had quite a nice place but it was at the top of a Victorian building, the good news was the hallway was very large at the entrance and we were allowed to leave the pram down there. Of course I changed my job yet again and became a trainee manageress at a Lavelles sweet and tobacco shop in Kensington Church Street. I took to it like a duck to water and before long they were sending me off to do relief managing to cover holidays at shops all over London of course this didn't suit me with my small time attitude towards work and travelling to get there. When they wouldn't give me a shop of my own to manage I set about looking for a new job with better prospects. I applied and got a job at a Jewish bakers called Grodinskis as a trainee manageress and they assured me that as soon as my training was complete they would give me a shop of my own to manage, the money and the prospects seemed good so I accepted and of course was on the move again This time to Cricklewood which was the nearest I could get to Willesden where my new job was, it wasn't ideal but would suffice until I had my own shop to manage.

While all this was going on my mum had found herself a girlfriend and seemed very happy. They also made a move to a much more upmarket place in West Hampstead, it was a self-contained flat above shops in

West End Lane. My friend Chris moved in to share with them and my mum who had to be interviewed to get the flat dug out her ladylike clothes again to pose as the matronly woman with her two daughters! Otherwise she would never have been considered. Everything seemed ok for them but apparently they had quite a stormy relationship. One day mum turned up at our place a little the worse for wear ostensibly to visit us and the baby but when I rang her flat they'd had a bust up and please send her home, so I poured her into a taxi gave him the address and the fare and sent her on her way. Problems arose when she fell to sleep in the back and he couldn't wake her he drove her to the local police station which was just up the road and while he was in there telling his story she woke up felt sick and lurched out of the cab and was sick on the pavement outside the station. They came out and arrested her for being drunk and incapable which swiftly changed to drunk and disorderly when they tried to put her in a cell, then she carried on so much that they searched her and found half a Dexedrine pill in her pocket it so they charged her with having drugs as well. By the time I found out I thought I'd better hurry up and get there before the list got any longer, so they let me bail her out. When she appeared in court they bound her over to keep the peace and she was given a fine.

It wasn't to be our last brush with the law, it turned out her girlfriend had a split personality which none of us knew about in the first place. She came across as quite posh, really well spoken and well turned out, as was her mother who we all met, she was a lovely lady and seemed really pleased that she was in a settled relationship with my mum, which was a bit strange for that day and age and most peoples attitude to homosexuality. All of a sudden Ann started coming home with loads of clothes, which in itself wasn't strange, but six skirts all the same in different sizes was. She was shoplifting but not the odd thing but lots of the same item in the hope that one of them may fit her, inevitably she was caught, it was at a food store and when it came up in court the magistrate said "I can understand someone taking food if they are hungry but what on earth did you want with nine different types of cheese?" Ann said "well my butch likes cheese and I didn't know which one she would prefer so I took them all!" So another fine to pay. We then found out that she had some mental issues and also had a child who was in a home, my mum started enquiries and a social worker came to assess my mum and the home situation with a view to my mum perhaps fostering the child if the relationship was stable enough. They were allowed to have her for days out, she was a lovely child about a year older than Wendy who was now toddling so we all had some nice times together going to the park having picnics, nice normal things to do. Then one time Ann went off with Mandy and was found shouting the odds like a fish wife and stripping her clothes off in an east end market. Obviously that put an end to any fostering plans and Ann ended up in a mental hospital in Kent for a while. That happened quite a while further into their relationship.

I had been given my very own shop to manage and it really was my very own as it was tiny and I was the only member of staff there! It was in Neasden and I managed to get us the top floor of a house just round the corner from the shop so it was ideal. The owner of the house lived downstairs and was a schoolteacher and we got on very well with her. I really enjoyed working there; all the regular customers were lovely and used to make a fuss of me. I was enjoying the challenge of doing all the bookwork and ordering myself, and some of the cakes they had were delicious much nicer than anything I'd ever had. The shop was long and quite narrow and my office at the back had a little hatch where I could watch out for customers as I was doing my paperwork or having something to eat as I couldn't just shut the shop and go home for dinner. One day I was sitting there eating my lunch it was a tin of baked beans and sausage on toast and who should walk through the door but the area supervisor, my desk had one of those really long drawers in it, I pulled it open and shot my lunch in there and slammed it shut, I couldn't really be caught eating pork sausages in a Jewish bakers it wouldn't be kosher. Well we greeted each other and I made him a cup of tea and we was just chatting in general all very nice until he said can I just have a look at your order form for next week as we have some new stuff to put on it, yes that's right it was in the long drawer which I very sheepishly opened felling quite sure I would get the sack. He roared with laughter when he saw what I'd done the blooming stuff was all over the paperwork. He forgave me but said just to have beans next time leave the sausage at home. Things seemed to be going really well, I had a job I enjoyed, Wendy had suddenly gone from being a cuddly little baby to a delightful three year old who everyone fell in love with. I had trouble prising her away from my nana when we managed to go to Fleetwood for a few days. Best of all was Jose seemed to have come out of her depression and had reverted to the lovely lass she was when we met. As soon as you become complacent some bastard sneaks up and kicks you in the backside! I don't know why but one day at work I suddenly felt the urge to go home, I put a sign on the shop door saying I'd be back soon and went home. It was really weird, everything to do with Jose and Wendy was gone, and it was as if they had never existed! Not even a farewell message. The cot, pushchair everything I just couldn't believe it. I went back to the shop on automatic pilot and rang the management to say I had a huge problem and could someone come and relieve me at the shop for a few days and they did, they were very understanding. Then went to my mum and Ann's and broke my heart, I knew I hadn't done anything wrong so couldn't even blame myself. Kathy the girl that had been with Jose the first time we met had turned back up but I had thought nothing about it, I didn't particularly like her but it wasn't up to me to choose José's' friends so I was in blissful ignorance of all the guff she was feeding to Jose. Some feelers were put out around the west end and eventually we found out that Kathy had taken her to Brighton to a person called Dee. This is where the salt really was rubbed in the wound apparently Jose really liked this Dee before she became pregnant and had been going out with her for a little while, when Dee found out she was pregnant she dropped her and moved on. It seems I looked very much like Dee so I was the second best thing! Information like that is really hard to swallow but quite apart from Jose I missed Wendy like mad I had been the main carer and it was like she was mine. I'd even managed to get José's father to see us and he had softened when he met Wendy as I thought he would, In fact he was so contented when we were there that he even managed his afternoon nap while we were chatting in the kitchen, when we went to waken him with a cup of tea it was hilarious, he had a wooden leg and a lump of coal had fallen into the hearth exactly where his foot was, so we had to douse his foot with water, that slowed him down till it was replaced. As more information came dribbling in from Brighton we found out that Dee had undergone a sex change, that was up to her/him, but also she was running a few girls on the game and my Jose was one of them. A little part of me thought it served her right but overall I was horrified and what was to become of little Wendy.

Some time passed and I'd given up my flat and moved in with my mum and Ann to help with the rent as Chris had gone back to live in Yorkshire, so I paid my third which was four guineas. Four pound four shillings if you're too young to remember the old money. I had also been promoted in my job and was now manageress of one of their main branches in Golders Green. Sounded good on the face of it but in reality I was in charge of seven staff the youngest one was seventy four and I was only about twenty two, how on earth could I ask them to do this that or the other, they were all a lot older than my nana! On top of that there was much more paperwork as we catered for lots of Bar mitzvahs and special occasions which all had to be worked out on bills and the payment was usually by cheque. As well as all that I wasn't sitting at home licking my wounds I was back on the rampage staying out all night drinking taking pep pills, I suppose I was also taking out my hurt and let down out on womankind, I don't think I was a very nice person for a while! One day Jose suddenly turned up out of the blue, My heart was racing I thought she wanted to come back, she said she was sorry for the way she had treated me and was sorry for the life she was now leading but couldn't see any easy way out of it, Dee seemed to have a terrible hold over her but she assured me that Wendy was alright. There wasn't much I could do It's not as if I could have claimed joint custody of Wendy I don't think that would even go down well in this day and age, so I just had to swallow it and get on with my life.

As usual it was very eventful, I asked a girl to dance one night which was unusual for me, it was a smoochy one and she seemed to be getting into it in a big way so

I asked her if she wanted to come home with me and she did She was in the bed before me and when I started to get undressed she gasped but didn't say anything, afterwards she said she'd thought I was a boy! The cause of the confusion turned out to be my hankie that was scrunched up in my pocket that was making her so hot she thought I had a hard on just from the dance, we had a good laugh about it and she seemed to have enjoyed what we did. I couldn't help liking her but she was to be in and out of my life like a yoyo. Once I was in bed with a woman I'd spent the night with and she walked in and said "hop it, that's my old man your with", the woman was petrified and fled without even a goodbye, I was gob smacked but could see the funny side of it and I suppose I was quite flattered. Then I found out where she was when she wasn't with me, her boyfriend was a small time gangster and apparently he was going round Soho asking who "Andy from Lancashire was?" I decided I would be "Eddie from Yorkshire" if anyone asked as he had supposedly said he was going to rip my head off when he found me. So quite a lot of ducking and diving went on till inevitably we met up. I walked into the Coffee Pot one night and the guy was sat at the bar with another bloke, it was too late to turn round and go plus I didn't think he knew what I looked like. As I arrived at the counter they got up and went, so thanking my lucky stars I went to sit on a bar stool and as I did saw a fiver on the floor I handed it over the bar to Charlie, good job I did the guy came back for it, on his own this time so perhaps it was a test to see what I would do. What I was doing was nearly wetting myself with fear; I quite liked my head and didn't want it ripped off! He bought a coffee sat next to me and said "well where is she?" I could have pretended not to know what he was talking about but thought what the hell and said "Why,

I thought she was with you!" Well He started laughing and I didn't know whether to laugh or cry, he said "she must be making mugs of us with someone else!" Strange things sometimes happen we got on very well, whether it was because we were fellow northerners I don't know but we became quite pally and used to meet up for drinks or go for a meal sometimes. One night we were walking up the mews to go for a meal somewhere and who should come round the corner but Bridget! Her face lit up ready to say hi and when she realised the two of us were there she went as white as a sheet we walked up linked her on either side and let her take the two of us for a meal.

Another thing that happened in that period of my life was quite alarming, we had been invited to a party somewhere in Chelsea we took a young woman with us who we didn't know very well but had asked could she come, anyway the party was in full swing in a small block of flats and we were enjoying ourselves (me and mum), when someone came and said was little Maria with us as she was out on the lawn downstairs hysterical and bleeding badly! We rushed down to see what had happened, my mum still clutching a bottle of wine. When we got there she had cut her wrists and made rather a good job of it if the amount of blood was anything to go by. A lady in the ground floor flat had rang for an ambulance and said we could bring her in if we wanted so we did, she was as light as a feather so I carried her in and the lady gave me a towel to staunch the blood flow, I had managed to calm her down though hadn't a clue why she'd done it. When the ambulance people came she went into hysteria again and wouldn't let them touch her, I asked if it was ok if I carried her into the ambulance and they said yes if I could manage it. So of course my mum got in as well and we all ended up going. When we arrived at the hospital as soon as they went to touch her she went hysterical again and was flailing about all over the place, the men in the ambulance allowed me to pick her up again and were guiding me down the steps when the driver who was a woman came and started tugging at her and saying it wasn't allowed She was nearly having us both over so I put Marie down and hauled a punch at the driver which made her stagger back picked Marie up and carried her into the hospital, in fact one of the staff led the way straight to a treatment room as she was bleeding so profusely. Marie actually allowed me to put her on the treatment bed, so apart from only being able to tell them her first name my part in all this was over. As I went out of the room my mum shouted RUN it's the old bill! It must have been like something out of a keystone cops movie, I ran one way my mum the opposite I soon came to the outside where the ambulance had dropped us and as I was running by I could hear someone snivelling behind the vehicle and it was the bloody driver, I wouldn't mind but she was huge and I was only eight stone wet through, I thought I'll give you something to cry for and whacked her again and that's when they caught me, they'd already nabbed my mum although she hadn't actually done anything, they then shoved us very unceremoniously into the back of their paddy wagon and of we went to the police station. When we got there I was putting up a bit of a fight as I didn't think I should be being arrested in the first place all I'd been doing was trying to help out till the driver started tugging me about, well I wasn't going to be calmed down and the upshot was they got very heavy with me pushing and punching me about, I ended up flat on my back spread eagled with a copper holding on to each arm and each leg the other one started to put his foot on my stomach my mum said I wouldn't do that if I was you she's got a duodenal ulcer, It shouldn't have taken five of them to restrain me anyway they were just enjoying bashing a lesbian about. They let me up and we were sat on a bench in the charge room and when I told them I needed the toilet they said I'd have to wait till they got a female copper in, by the time she came I was nearly exploding. Eventually they read the charge sheet out to me, I was being done for actual bodily harm to the driver, abusive language, resisting arrest and assaulting five police officers! No mention of the beating they had given me, I said I'm not signing that I would hold my hands up to the first three offences but if they wanted to charge me with the last they would have to get a doctor to examine me as I was black and blue all over my body (I had a look when I was in the toilet), earlier on that day I'd had a top to bottom medical with my doctor and he would be able to verify I had no bruising. Well they went off in a huddle and came back with a new charge sheet omitting the assault of five police officers so I was willing to sign it Then much to our amazement they stood my mum at the desk and charged her with assaulting five police officers it was laughable she was five foot four and eight stone they were all like giant rugby players, when she started to refuse to sign it they said they would have to lock her up in the holding cell, as she was claustrophobic she signed. They then let us out into the middle of god knows where in the early hours of the morning. We didn't even know what direction we should be going in but walked along thumbing a lift in the hope someone would stop and at least tell us where we were! Someone did stop and said jump in, we said we were heading for the west end, as we would be able to get home from there. Then my mum still clutching the bottle of wine we'd been given back said " you'll never guess what's just happened to us mate" He said "I know I was one of the cops I came to look for you as I think you had a raw deal" so at least there was one decent one amongst them. He dropped us off and we finished our strange night out in the Limbo. Eventually we had letters telling us when the case was to be held and where, but my mum had been in trouble before so she had to go and see someone for probation reports! When the case actually came to court half the people we knew in the club came to support as they thought we were getting a raw deal, thinking about it now I don't know what we thought would be helpful about a room full of prostitutes, drug addicts and fellow homosexuals! A bloke from the CID searched us out before we went in and said to us I don't know what you've done to upset them but it looks to me like your being railroaded, according to him the only thing that was going to be left for my mum was a prison sentence as they said she wouldn't be able to pay a fine was not likely to turn up for probation so a custodial sentence seemed to be the only option, we were amazed as in actuality she hadn't done anything except to be with me. He said he would speak up for us and he did, he implied that the ambulance driver was fiddling about with the patient when she was trying to get her out of my arms and that was why I'd hit her, my mum was an innocent bystander to all intents and purposes and had only got involved by trying to protect her daughter which was natural. Thankfully the sentence was light we were both bound over to keep the peace for twelve months and fined twenty-five pounds each. I thought my eyes were deceiving me when I saw the ambulance driver in court she was a huge butch number and had fetched up in a pale pink twin set and even had the pearls to go with, how I managed to stop myself giving her another whack I'll never know. The person we got into all that trouble for? We never laid eyes on her again!

When my mum's girlfriend had been caught doing something else illegal she was offered the option of going into a mental hospital for treatment as an alternative to going to prison, so she went to a place in Kent. We were fortunate to have someone give us a lift there to see her, The building was beautiful and in a lovely setting it was more like going to a stately home than a nuthouse, the day I went they were having some sort of a party for the inmates, some of whom were reasonably ok and some that were absolutely gone. There was a disco going on and sandwich's and soft drinks, so I mucked in and tried to help out in general while mum and Ann had a chat, the food was getting a bit low so I went to the kitchen to get some more, there was a nice young woman preparing everything and we got talking, she said she would be in London at the weekend and perhaps we could meet up for a drink. I thought that was a great idea and gave her my phone number. Later on we were allowed to take Ann to the local pub for an hour or so as she was considered well on the road to recovery, with the help of medication. Whilst we were chatting I told them I'd copped off with this lovely lady in the kitchen who was going to meet me at the weekend, Ann described her exactly and I said she was right all proud of myself, she said "I hope you haven't given her your address, she's been in here for two years and was in for stabbing her girlfriend in the back!" thank goodness I'd only dished out the phone number! When Ann came home she was alright for a little while but never seemed properly settled and eventually they split up and she left, there was no big drama's or anything it was just time to end it. Mum was more gutted for what might have been had everything been right. We wasn't really in to banks in those days so used to put our rent aside in a cupboard and go and pay it monthly to the landlord, it was quite a hefty amount to have around but we trusted each other not to dib in to it. We came back from being out one day and the tenant above us who rarely spoke said "it was nice to see Ann again she's not been around much lately has she?" When we got in we expected to see her sitting there but the first thing we saw was the cupboard door wide open and the money gone. When we checked with the neighbour again there was another girl with her, we recognised who it was from his description, it was Sheila Samid a girl Chris used to go out with at one time. We went to Soho that night to try and find out if anyone knew anything and we were told they were heading to Birmingham where Sheila was from originally. We were fuming we stayed out till the coaches started running from Victoria in the morning and set off to Birmingham to try and find them. We did have an old address of Sheila's dad so we were hopeful we would track them down. I have to say by the time we arrived we were stoned out of our minds on pep pills and must have looked it. We landed up in the bullring and went and asked a policeman for directions, he said "the only directions I'll give you two is right back to wherever you've come from", Lovely greeting, anyway we eventually found our way to the area only to discover the whole street and a few more had been demolished and everyone had been rehoused so someone suggested we go and enquire at the local post office which amazingly was still there. When we asked him if he could tell us where they may have been moved to he cracked out laughing and said "do you know how many Samid's there are in Birmingham it's a bit like Smith or Jones there's millions of them" it made it worse as he was a Pakistani his self wouldn't have been surprised if he was called Samid as well. So that was a futile exercise but we did manage to find our way to a bar that was mainly frequented by gays so we stayed there for a while to drown our sorrows. Met up with some friendly folk and before we knew it realised we'd missed the last coach. Found our way to the railway station and tried to explain at the ticket office what had happened and could we give our details get a ticket and pay it back when we got home, apparently you couldn't do it that way but if you got on the train anyway you could give your details to the ticket inspector when he came round, seemed a dodgy way to do it but we weren't in a position to argue, as we set off to go to the platform about three lads run past us nearly knocking me over and as I turned to see where they went I found myself flat on the floor with someone trying to put handcuffs on me, the officer chasing the lads obviously thought I was one of them, they wouldn't let me go till they went back to the ticket office to confirm my story. All in all a terrible twenty-four hours and we had even less money than in the first place. The good news was there wasn't a ticket inspector on the train and there was no one at the barrier when we got off, so we'd tried to be honest and it didn't work but we were better off because of it.

Trying to pull back forty eight guineas was crippling with only two of us and of course we did what millions of people have done before us, didn't like to tell them we hadn't got the full money so didn't give them any thinking we would catch up but never did.

Previous to all this being in charge of all the old girls at the shop had got the better of me and I'd ended up collapsing and being took out on a stretcher that's when I discovered I had a duodenal ulcer, don't suppose my lifestyle was helping things. When I'd recovered a little I went back to say I couldn't carry on and would have to leave, a shame really, as it was a good job and apart from all the old girls I loved it. They knew I was coming in that day and old Mr Grodinzky, his son and grandson came down to try and convince me not to leave, he must have been about ninety and apologised for leaving me in charge of such aging staff but wanted to hand over to the likes of me and his Great grandson Reuben. I said thanks but no thanks and that was that. I found myself for the first time ever properly out of work and having to sign on at the dole, my mum had been doing it for years, and I don't know how she got away with not finding a job for so long.

Somewhere along the line mum found a new light of her life, unfortunately for all of us she was a heroin addict, but I suppose its hard to choose who you fall for. You think you can cope with an addict and if they care about you enough they'll come off it, the addict thinks so too in between fixes but as soon as it starts wearing off they want more. I had a little experience with junkies as a couple of social workers started coming down the club in the hope of offering help to addicts and runaways, they found they wasn't making any headway but had obviously watched the interaction between mum and myself with people who were in trouble. If we could help them we did, sometimes we would see a youngster down the club obviously for the first time all wide eyed and excited to be alive, dancing the night away. The next night they would be sitting quietly in the corner not interacting at all and the third night you would find them snuggled up in the darkest corner of the club trying to get to sleep and looking decidedly scruffy, as they would be wearing the same clothes they started off in. We quite often used to scoop these kids up and take them home with us for a bath a sleep and a change of clothes as well as a couple of decent meals. If we could persuade them to get in touch with their family we did and they quite often came and collected them, otherwise we used to scrape together to give them coach fare home and hope that's where they went. Quite often some of the people who were starting to take the hard stuff were one's that had been friends with us in the first place and only used to pop a few pills but had got curious and drifted in to taking the hard stuff, they were easily led into it funnily enough by the people who were on it themselves but wishing they weren't, I could never get to grips with it and was never in the least bit tempted. Some of the nurses at the local hospital started calling me Dr Kildare as I used to take these girls that I found slumped in the gutter with an overdose in for treatment. Anyway one of the social workers approached me and said "we have been watching how you and your mum and people seem to come to you two for help much more than they do with us, would you be prepared to help us?" so we did, instead of trying to sort it out ourselves we would guide some of the lasses towards the social worker and hope that they sorted them out, this arrangement went on for a good while. My mum's girlfriend was well and truly hooked and would do anything to get drugs. There was a guy who provided them but if she had no money would set her up with punters for sex to get the wherewithal to buy the drug, we were robbed blind and didn't even have any money for food most of the time. We managed to get hold of her sister up north who came down with her boyfriend to try and help, they ended up living with us as well and the sister managed to get a job in a small local grocery shop and took most of her wages in food so it couldn't be stolen for heroin. Nothing we did or tried to do helped, of course my mum blamed the whole thing on the sleaze ball that was providing the drugs and putting her on the game. One night I hadn't gone out and in the early hours had a phone call from the guy who managed the Limbo, he said you'd better get down here and find your mum she has a gun and is looking for Paula's pimp. I didn't believe my ears, anyway I got down there and couldn't find her in any of our usual haunts, had half of Soho looking for her, eventually found her sitting on a doorstep down an alley crying, I thought she'd done the deed but she was crying because she hadn't found him, I felt through her pockets for the gun but she said she'd dumped it in one of the huge bins the clubs and restaurants used, so there was no way I could get it back. She had found out who to get one off and the deal was if she didn't use it she could just give it back but if it was used she had to pay the fee and get rid of it! The good news was it was a gangster with a heart that she got it from and he let her off. Not long afterwards Paula's sister managed to whisk her away back to their home town, my mum was gutted but I was relieved as I'd had enough of her shenanigans.

Meanwhile we weren't doing any better on the rent department and both of us were still out of work. My mum was acting out and drinking a lot again as well as taking pills, somehow she managed to put her foot through the bedroom window in one of her rants it was no mean feat as it was four foot from the floor, I wasn't there when she did it but can only assume she was contemplating jumping out of it at the time. She couldn't remember a thing the next day but the ankle was in a really bad way. I got the doctor out and he sent her straight to a hospital in ST Johns Wood. It turned out to be run by nursing nuns and was also where nuns were admitted to if they were ill there were other patients there some private and some like my mum who had nothing. A real strange place for my mum to end up, but the foot was really badly infected and she was delirious most of the time for the first few days, they said afterwards she was lucky not to have lost the foot, they operated on it and saved it but she was in there quite a while and a least she got chance to dry out from the booze. I had enough of all the worry by this time so I prevailed on some friends to look after our stuff and vacated our flat in West Hampstead, locked it all up and put the keys and a very apologetic letter in the mailbox. I hadn't really thought it through, mum was ok in hospital, our belongings even had a home but I didn't. The first couple of nights were all right hanging around the Limbo as usual all night then I was turning up at the hospital in the morning and strangely enough they let me in. I don't know what the poor nuns must have been thinking me turning up in full drag all the time, I even had a crombie overcoat and a trilby but not even an eyebrow was raised. When my mum started to become a bit more compus- mentis she started saving me her boiled egg from her breakfast as I wasn't eating, when they realised what she was doing they started giving her two, they really were very sweet. The other funny thing was some of the nuns that came for treatment thought my mum was a nun because of her short hair, I don't know what they do now but in those days they all had short hair. Once she was feeling better she had them in stitches and I think they were quite enjoying the experience, they'd also started talking about things they liked when they were kids so I ended up talking things like jelly babies and liquorice comfits in. One of the nuns who belonged to the order little sisters of the poor, took a shine to me and one day put her hands around my face and looked at me and said "sure, you'd make a lovely nun and would look beautiful in a wimple", it took every bit of my will power not to wet myself laughing. Whilst mum was in there it was my birthday and I went in as usual and they all sang happy birthday to me, and I was given lots of little gifts, silly things but all the more touching for their simplicity one lady, not a nun had made a lovely rose out of tissue paper and wrapped it round a two shilling piece, I was really touched by it all, nowhere to live, no money, my mum in hospital and nowhere to come out to yet it was one of the nicest birthdays I'd had.

As I'd been down the club even more than usual for me Alex the owner took me to one side and asked me what was the matter, when I explained it all he told me off for not letting him know and took me to his flat across the road and sorted me out with a bed and a change of clothes much like we had done for all the runaways, said I was to stay with him till we could sort something out, I was really grateful. The next day he insisted on coming with me to the hospital so we went later in the day and a couple of his henchmen came too. It was very funny seeing them surrounded by nuns when they would have been happier marching round with sawn off shotguns they looked very out of place marching down the ward with a huge bouquet of flowers a big bowl of fruit. He was my saviour; he lent me some money to get a flat, so at least I could get a new start. I found one in Clapham South, a ground floor one so jumping out of the window wouldn't be an option if my mum went off on one again. It wasn't as splendid as our last one but at least we could afford the rent, it was a bed-sitter and kitchen again but seemed like heaven to me.

So everything back on an even keel, mum was let out of hospital and was pleased with the place. I had managed to get a job at Vauxhall Motors, that was different, we had to clean the wax covering from the cabs that would pull heavy goods loaders, it was an onerous job as it was wax laid on thick to protect them for all the time they stood outside the manufacturers waiting to be sold. The really good part of the job that I enjoyed was doing up second hand cars and making them look like new again, there was a lot of job satisfaction in that and even better, when they were sold we had a percentage of the profit which was often more than our wages, by this time I was earning about fifteen pounds a week about six times more than my first job in Fleetwood. I paid Alex back straight away which made me feel loads better. Vauxhalls was at Kennington and just across the road was a gay pub that we started using, well I suppose it was mixed as some nights it had drag shows and others a stripper, we didn't know what was on and one night we turned up when it was the stripper, well I'd never seen one before so I suppose I must have been looking a bit goggle eyed, as she divested herself of all her clothes, very artistically I thought, she threw them all at me, everybody that knew me were tickled pink as they knew I was a girl she obviously didn't! We did have a laugh about it after and she took it quite well. Then another night when the drag show was on he lunged forward and dragged my mum up on the stage thinking she was a bloke and started stripping her, his face was a picture when he realised there were boobs under the waistcoat but he still carried on but kept her back to the audience to spare her blushes and his. We had some good nights in there; it was also very handy for me at my lunch breaks. They took a young lad on as an apprentice he was only fifteen he asked me where I went at lunchtimes one day so I said he could come with me if he wanted, he was really chuffed being taken to the pub at dinner time, anyway we was a bit late back and Bert my boss said "get in my car" well he used it as his office and I thought I was in for a telling off for being late or taking the youngster to the pub, he told me to take him where we had been, when we got there the bosses son was there behind the bar but to be fair he didn't look like any ones son just like a very pretty girl. He had a mass of fair curls, nail varnish, make up and a flowery blouse. When Bert went to get the drinks I gave the boy a wink and he made a real fuss of Bert who came back to the table all but drooling. He didn't believe me when I said it was a boy he was dribbling over, he led a very sheltered life but was fascinated by it all. The boy became a very well-known drag Queen and as far as I know was still performing about ten years ago as I saw a billboard in Manchester for Miss Candy Du Barry. I doubt if he would have remembered me but it was nice to see he was still going strong.

While still working there I scalded my foot with hot fat and it took bad ways as it landed on an old scald from when I was little so I had to attend the hospital quite regularly, Bert took it upon himself to take me then on the way back we would go to The Vauxhall tavern or the Elephant and Castle at Vauxhall as it was on the way back, there wasn't anything very different about the pubs in daytime but because he knew they had drag shows at night he was thrilled to be there and I used to just tell him stories about it, he had a mentally sick wife at home so didn't manage to get out at night, he was a lovely man.

While we lived at Clapham my mum seemed to be going through a different faze of self-hate and was forever making out she was going to top herself either with overdoses of tablets or chucking herself under a car, all very dramatic but she never actually intended to carry it through. My patience was wearing very thin, I didn't even know what the reason was either and I don't think she did if the truth were known. One night a couple of gay guys gave us a lift back from the pub and were going to stay for coffee. They had a funny shaped little van taller than it was wide and I was curious about it, when we got home they opened up the back part to show me, they were in the rag trade and had this special part of the van with all their samples hung up a very clever way of storing the dresses without getting them screwed up. When we got in my mum was missing, I didn't think too much about it she would come back when she was ready, we were having our coffee and a chat when the phone rang, it was a shared house phone up on the landing. I went to answer it never dreaming it would be for me. It was the night sister from the ladies hospital at the top of the road, it was my mum up to her old tricks and had told the nurse she had taken an overdose, she didn't believe her either since she had been so keen to give them my number, and would I come and collect her? No you found her so you can keep her I was thoroughly pissed off with her and just didn't want to know. About an hour later I had another call to say she'd been taken to Tooting Bec hospital to the psychiatric department. I was relieved maybe they could get to the bottom of what was ailing her, my guests left and I went to bed. I let her stew for a couple of days then went up to see her, she hadn't learnt any lessons, was absolutely full of herself saying the doctor had said she was more sane than her! Plus she'd made friends with some off the other inmates and seemed relatively happy to stay where she was. When I came in from work a couple of days later she was home, she had been discharged the only trouble was she had a couple of women with her who were obviously loony tunes. I rang the hospital and asked them if anything was missing and they came and collected them in a white van, I always thought that was just in films. My mum wasn't stupid she'd brought them out with her because they gave her the stash of pills they'd been collecting. What she didn't take she sold that night in the Limbo. I wasn't a paragon of virtue I enjoyed popping a few pills with the rest of them but I think the novelty was wearing of and I was getting ready for a change. I had a mate who had come from Birmingham for the bright lights of London and discovered she wasn't as impressed as she thought she would be, so when I mentioned I was thinking of leaving she asked could she come with me. I decided on Manchester I'd had a couple of weekends there in the past and I knew a woman that lived there who may point us in the direction of bed-sit land Manchester style. I told Bert a bit of a fib so I could pick all my money up at once, holiday pay and such, so that was that. Telling my mum wasn't that simple but I made sure the rent was paid a couple of weeks in advance and the food cupboard was stacked. She didn't gripe too much I think she realised it was her that was getting me down.

Manchester

Well we arrived in the early afternoon and before ringing Rene, my friend we put our belongings in left luggage as we didn't want to be dragging that round with us whilst flat hunting. Rene was another little story all by herself; I met her in Yates Wine Lodge in Blackpool not long after my discharge from the army. I had been to the toilet and as usual there was a queue so a few of us got talking about nothing in particular and I thought no more about it. About half an hour before closing time a lady came over and said my friend over there would like to speak to you, so full of beer and bravado I went over, I recognised her as one of the ladies in the loo and she asked me would I like to go to a party, I said yes but I was with my pal and my mum could they come as well? She didn't really want to take the Mickey, as it wasn't her home the party was in so better not. I went and said ta-ra to my mum and Jill and of we went to this party. Rene was an older lady more my mums age and I was quite impressed that she had invited me, she seemed posh as well probably a bit up market for me, but I thought what the heck this may be my moment! I wasn't so impressed when I got there, the 'party 'was in full swing and was a mixture of gay men and women, they were nearly all playing spin the bottle and in varying stages of undress! I fled to another room wondering what on earth I'd got myself into. Rene followed me and was very apologetic and said her friends weren't usually like that and she was mortified. Anyway she drove me home in her little bubble car and I was nearly back at the same time as mum and Jill. I did arrange to meet her again on her own in a pub in Blackpool and we had a very civilised evening with no more than a bit of hand holding and a quick kiss when she dropped me off, she told me most of her friends that had been at the party were solicitors, teachers and the like I wasn't sure if I was supposed to be impressed or I was a bit of rough. She did invite me to another party and as we'd had a pleasant evening agreed to go. This time it seemed a fairly normal do with plenty of drink flowing music and dancing, everyone seemed friendly, except one butch who wasn't very nice at all, Rene said she lived near her in Manchester and had thought she would be Rene's partner for the party and just to ignore her which I did. Well somehow or other we ended up sliding into another room together and more or less found our way to the bed. I thought my luck was in, but she didn't want to kiss and cuddle first just wanted to get on with it, seeing as I hadn't actually done "IT" before it more or less turned in to a wrestling match with her making grabs and lunges, I was horrified luckily for me someone came in and put the light on and I was gob smacked to see at least three other couples writhing around on the floor! If this was sophisticated living I wanted none of it and Rene had given me the horrors. I was taken home once again, I was anything but a prude though I thought there was a time and place for everything she apologised once again and I thought that was that. A couple of weeks later I had a letter from her saying she was going to have a big operation and would be staying at her friends to recover would I consider visiting her, to cut a long story short I did and we became friends rather than lovers. So I wasn't quite sure what my reception would be like when I rang to ask advice on where it was best to look for a flat as I hadn't seen her for years and only made the odd phone call usually when I was stoned out of my mind.

When I rang she asked where I was and said she would come and pick me up, I hastily told her I had a pal with me in case she got the wrong idea, that was

fine she said " as long as I hadn't gone all London",
whatever that meant. When she arrived she made us get
our luggage back out and took us home. She had a
lovely flat, the whole ground floor of a big Victorian
house and beautiful gardens, looked lovely after being
in London and only living in bed-sits. After we had
something to eat she took us round the corner where
she knew a flat was coming up. The landlord was
actually in the flat decorating it and it looked lovely, I
thought I'll never get this it will be too expensive but of
course after the prices in London it seemed cheap six
pounds a week. It was a converted coal cellar that the
previous landlord had been doing up for his self but had
a heart attack and died before completing it, he said I
could move in a week later, Rene said we could stay
with her till then, I'd only been in Manchester a few
hours and already had my own place, I was thrilled.
The next day I went out armed with directions on how
to get to town from where I was, found my way to
Victoria and blow me down I got the first job I tried for
which was a petrol pump attendant, they said I could
start the next day, my pal wasn't so lucky but at least
one of us was working. I think Rene was very
impressed as well, which was good seeing as she was
putting us up.

Well I settled in to a relatively calm way of life, my
flatmate had a sister who came to visit and shortly after
and she decide to go back to Birmingham as she was
homesick. I had a phone call from a friend who said my
mum had tried her suicide bids again but I took no
notice and didn't mention anything in my letters so if it
was directed at me it fell on stony ground. My job at
the garage was quite eventful, I hadn't had much to do
with cars except for the ones I cleaned at my last job, so
checking oil and water was a mystery to me I was only
just managing to put the petrol in. It was at a time when

you did it all for the customer, one chap gave me his keys and wanted it filling up it was a foreign looking car and he implied it was in the boot! So I'm looking askance in the boot and thought oh good there it is, put the nozzle in and locked it on whilst I went to check the oil and water, I heard a shout from my boss in the shop part and looked down the forecourt was flooding with petrol, I'd only put the nozzle in the hole were the lock was! Fortunately they thought it was funny, not to mention stupid. Whenever I tried to do any ones tyres I used to let more air out than I put in, I didn't like the hissing sound it made (so brave). There were two different banks of pumps, one lot had three, four and five star petrol, the other had diesel and two star, where the big wagons and motorbikes filled up. So when a taxi driver parked his black cab there and asked to be filled up, I did, the problem was I did it with two star petrol! I didn't think cars had diesel in them. Oh boy, I was sure this must be a sacking offence as the whole thing had to be drained, cleaned out and then the diesel put in. The cab driver was a mate of my boss so wasn't as annoyed as he could have been, also the boss seemed to have taken a shine to me, which was just as well I must have been costing him a fortune.

I arrived home from work one evening to see loads of tea chests near where the dustbins were situated I thought someone must have moved in upstairs, as I opened my door there was a telegram on the floor, from my mum, "arriving Chorlton street coach station six thirty please meet me, mum", Grrrr, I'd just come home from that direction and there was no way I could get back there in twenty minutes, good old Rene helped me out once again and took me to pick her up. I was furious it was like having a permanent shadow; I loved her to bits but would have liked a life of my own. Most parents try to get their kids to leave the nest at some stage; I was expected to feather the nest for my mum. When we got home and Rene had left I decided a stern conversation was required, I've never done anything so stupid in my life, I told her she could stay with me for the time being but if I found myself a girlfriend she would have to leave and get a place of her own, worst thing I could have said, any time I so much as looked at someone she would do her best scupper any chance of a relationship. Having said that we did have some fun in Manchester, we used to mainly drink in the Union and the New York and we made a lot of friends, one in particular was going to be our best mate, the three of us used to nearly always be together they called us the three musketeers. A lot of the girls that frequented the Union were on the game and used it as a picking up place, so when they went to 'do' one they would leave their handbags with us for safety, I seemed to spend most of my time clutching a handbag, which didn't go very well with a suit and tie. They always bought us a drink when they came back which was handy as we never really had much money, again I was the only one working, well with a straight job anyway. I had moved on from the garage with no hard feelings the boss was a lovely man and though I must have cost him a fortune he still said he'd miss me, I think mainly from an entertainment point of view. I had a job at Trafford warehouse in the demand booking office, where the majority of the catalogues went out. I couldn't believe the amount of false names they sent stuff out to they must have lost loads of money, when I said as much to one of the supervisors she looked at me as if I was daft obviously didn't have a mind like mine, a few names, C Hunt, S Tink, B Ugger, they quite happily sent hundreds of pounds worth of goods out to these people. During this period of time the great power switch off happened, it made life interesting, I used to manage to have a hot drink before leaving for work and leave home in blackness, we had emergency generated power at work so no stoppage there. My mum used to have cooked a dinner in the afternoon when the power was on then wrap it up in tea towels to keep it warm for me getting in. We had a hot drink out of a flask then had to get ready to go to town in the dark, all we had for warmth was a little paraffin heater that took the chill off but stank to high heaven. We used to just about manage to get in the pub and their power would go off, but they had rigged up big powerful gaslights and there was always a party atmosphere, when we arrived at the pub we often discovered we had odd socks on once we even had on of each other's shoes on. Everyone pulls together in adversity and good times were had by all. One night we were in the pub and sharing a table with a couple of strangers from the north east judging by their accents, anyway they were likely lads and we were having a laugh, we even shared some of our pep pills with them. At closing time we decided to go to a club they asked could they come with us, when we got there and were signing in ready to pay our jaws nearly hit the floor when they said there's no need to pay and flashed their warrant cards, we had latched on to two coppers fortunately for us they were off duty.

One night we were taken to a Shebeen, we didn't even know what it was till we got there, it's just someone using their home as a late night illegal drinking place, it made a change from the usual club and we had a good night so decided to go again the next night. There was another girl with us who had just come out of prison, Marge knew her so the four of us set off with high hopes of another good night. The cab dropped us of in the avenue we had been in the night before; we couldn't see sight or sign of the place. The night before we had been able to hear the music as we got out of the cab, so we were walking up the avenue checking all the basements to see if we could hear any signs of life, some old girl opened her window upstairs and asked what we thought we were doing, so we said looking for a club. Further up the avenue we saw a couple getting out of a car so two of us ran up to ask if they knew where it was and as we were doing that we turned round to see a Black Maria full of cops dragging my mum and Marge's friend into the back, we shot back to say we were only looking for a club not doing anything wrong but they wouldn't listen and bundled us in as well. When we got to the police station they said there wasn't a club down the avenue and charged us all with "loitering with intent" the only intent we had was having a late drink. In the evening paper the next day was a story about the police raiding the place they told us didn't exist, it had happened about an hour before our arrival. So we held on to it and when we had to attend court in front of a magistrate called Nelly Beer of all things we presented the cutting as evidence that we were looking for a specific place and not loitering, she let us off and said we should avoid going to illegal drinking clubs.

During that time my mum had to have a hysterectomy as she suddenly started haemorrhaging rather badly. They kept trying to admit her for the operation but every time she was so short of blood they just gave her a transfusion and sent her home, in the end they admitted her and gave her the transfusion and then operated on her the next day. It didn't go all that well as she had been weakened through all the times she had been losing so much blood, she was on what they called 'the free list 'which meant there was every possibility she could die. Before the operation she had made me promise not to tell anyone in the family so that my nana didn't get worried. It was a very stressful time and she was on the free list for nine days, I think I knew every nurse in the hospital I spent so much time there, work was very good with allowing me time to go and be with her. It took her a little while to recover but she bounced back as usual.

Whilst I working at the warehouse I used to bring homework back with me, it boosted my wage a bit as you were paid so much a hundred for putting paper work in envelopes, so my mum and anyone who happened to be around helped me with this but my mum felt it necessary to look at each address and read it instead of just making sure it showed through the window in the envelope. When she found any from Fleetwood she would say oh I know her or I used to go to school with her brother and one day I just managed to stop her putting a note in with the bill saying "how are you doing, do you remember me?" She could have got me sacked!

The job was all right but it was very boring to say the least so I always had a look in the job section of the local paper just in case there was something interesting. One day I saw an advert for a fire woman! I had never heard of a fire woman so it piqued my curiosity and I sent for an application form. When it came my heart sank it was huge, they wanted to know all the jobs you had ever done I thought they'd take one look at my very long list and read no further but the worst part was having to say if you were in the forces and reason for discharge. I had tried for better jobs before and they wanted to see my discharge book and that used to be the end of it as it said "discharged in the interest of the WRAC" enough to make any one's mind boggle I could have been a spy or anything! So in the box provided wrote I would explain at interview and just prayed that someone would be curious enough to want to find out. Amazingly I was offered an interview; I was very nervous as well as excited I really wanted this job. When I saw the officer that was to conduct the interview I thought well it's no good lying about anything to this lady, she had the most piercing blue eye's that made you think she could look inside you and see your soul. Well I told her everything warts and all, how I made a nuisance of myself to get out and why. When I'd finished she leant forward and said, "Well whatever else you have been up to you are extremely honest". I thought that's it I've blown it I shouldn't have told her as much as I did. Two weeks later I had a letter saying I'd got the job, our postman used to come early so it was before I went to work. I was absolutely bursting with joy, I had a big daft grin on my face and I found myself telling everyone on the bus, a couple of them may have known me but the rest must have thought I was nuts!

I enjoyed my time in the fire brigade; it was just before they let women go out on calls so my job was in the control room. It was a bit daunting at first as the action you took with a call could be the difference between life and death. There were some very sad times when people had been killed and I've seen many a big strong fireman break down in tears when they got back. There were also some comical events, one day I answered a call and a nearly hysterical lady with a very posh voice said " please you must help me, my pussy is stuck on a bridge", it may not come through as funny written down but you can imagine what the picture that flitted through my mind was like. Another call was again about a cat, the chap said he wasn't sure it was us he should have called but a young cat had been stuck up his very large tree for a couple of days and he was worried about it, fair enough I rang the police station who gave me a number of an animal rescue group which I passed on to him, he thanked me profusely and off he went. About two hours later the same chap rang again and this time he was peeing himself laughing, the chap from the rescue came but now he was stuck up the tree as well! So because it was a person stuck up the tree we were allowed to respond this time, they got the chap down and radioed in to let us know they were returning to station, about half an hour later they radioed in to say they were mobile to the last incident as they'd left some equipment behind. When they returned to the station the sub officer rang to tell us what had happened, they got the man down but the cat had gone much further up the tree because they weren't allowed to go up just for the cat for insurance purposes they left the ladder behind so the guy could get up high enough to get the cat! All was well when they went back. Another incident that on the face of it was quite funny but it turned out to be sad, a woman rang to say that her and her boyfriend were in bed having sex and one of the coiled springs in the mattress had come through the material and stuck right through his calf and they couldn't move, as you can imagine a fair amount of sniggering occurred in the control room and it was an appliance from our station that went out as it was local so we were waiting with bated breath for them to come back and tell all. They did but it wasn't a bit of fun as we expected, when the address was given on the way to the shout it turned out it was one of the crew members home they were heading to so you can imagine the scene when he got there and even worse it was a bloke from another station who was with his wife and he'd thought he was a mate! He removed the spring from the bed none too carefully and the bloke was taken to hospital, the husband was left behind to try and sort things out. He never did and they ended up getting divorced.

Meanwhile I was still on a quest to find myself a nice girlfriend, it never came off as every time I looked like I was taking more than a passing interest in someone my mum leapt into action and did everything she could to put a spanner in the works so she wouldn't have to move out. I went out with one woman for a while and we had a few giggles but nothing too serious, she had a red mini car and spent half her time looking for it, every time we went for a night out she'd park it behind the Union and every closing time it was missing! The first couple of times she reported it to the police but when it kept turning back up in the car park they thought she was having a laugh so we didn't bother any more. Eventually we caught the girl that was doing it, she said it was dead easy to get into the mini, so she used to borrow it for the night to go and see her girlfriend who lived about thirty miles away then put it back in the early hours of the morning.

I did start seeing a girl who lived locally, she used to sing in the pub we sometimes went to, anyway one thing led to another and we ended up having a fling. She was basically straight and I think she only got involved with me out of curiosity. She was also a bit of a girl it turned out, she used to say she was working late and would stagger in drunk and say they all went to the pub after, it was a bit thin to say the least, anyway when she staggered in another night with grass stains all over her dress I gave her marching orders. She wasn't too thrilled at being told to go and said she would tell them all about me at my work, I was genuinely worried as that would have cost me my job in those days. Turns out she was a bit of a nut job as well she ran in front of the bus I was on and he had to do an emergency stop. I had to confide in one of my fellow workers and she said she would man the switchboard and if the girl rang she would pretend to be my group officer. The woman did ring and Dianna saved the day for me.

One day out of the blue I had a phone call (at home) from Jose, I couldn't believe I was talking to her all the old feelings came flooding back. She said she had been trying to find me for ages had even put an advert in the paper I used to read and in the end she had a friend she knew drive her all the way from Shoeberryness to my nanas in Fleetwood. Of course my nana remembered her and Wendy so she gave her my number and address. She asked could she come for a visit. Of course I was thrilled and yet didn't really know what to expect, looking forward to seeing my little Wendy who would be a proper little girl now seven years old. She came and we all had three glorious weeks, it was as if we'd never been apart, she was very reticent about what she had been up to, but what's the good of raking old coals, I was as happy as a sand boy. We arranged a visit at her place and as soon as I could arrange some holidays we went to stay with her. For once I was really pleased I'd taken my mum with me! It was a totally different woman to the carefree one that had stayed with me for three lovely weeks. She was acting really strange convinced she was being followed. On the odd occasion we could get her outdoors and when she was in she kept peeping through the curtains all the time. In fairness she was really good with Wendy but she definitely seemed to be undergoing some form of paranoia. She was acting as if nothing had gone on between us when she came to visit us in Manchester it was like she was a completely different person, strange. She did take us to a pub and introduced us to a gay boy she knew then said look after them and left? I just couldn't understand it at all, why go to all the trouble of finding me then carrying on like that? The gay boy said he had known her for a while but she had just gone funny in the last few months and he couldn't understand it either.

Well we headed off to London with the young man and at some stage he met up with someone and left us to our own devices. We decided to see how the Gateway was doing in our absence, not that it was a favourite of mine I found it to be a bit clicky on the occasions I went there but mum liked it. Funnily enough it was about to start the next big milestone in my life. It was quite busy that night and who should we bump into but the girl from Manchester who kept getting her car stolen, she was with her new girlfriend and had moved in with her in London, it is a small world and on the gay scene especially at that time it was even smaller. They were with another group of people and they were all going on to another club later on, we were worried if we did we wouldn't get back but the two girls said they would put us up so off we went. The club had the unlikely name of "Shagerama's," I have to say in all the years I lived in London afterwards I never found it again, no one had ever heard of it but believe me it was definitely there it wasn't a mirage. It was a massive place with a big dance area but if you weren't in to the music and dancing you could sit far enough away to hear each other speak but still watch all the action. I wasn't very into bopping about and found myself sitting next to Milly, she sparkled in every sense of the word she was half caste which tended to make her jewels stand out even more but her personality sparkled even more. As you can gather I was quite taken with her. We got talking and it turned out her mum lived in Manchester and she used to visit often so perhaps we could meet up for a night out in Manchester. I thought that would be great, she seemed to have a girlfriend with her, not that we saw much of her as she was mainly on the dance floor. Milly gave me her phone number and said if I rang, to do a code, let it ring three times then stop and ring it again so she'd know it was me, a bit strange but intriguing anyway we had a really good night and did stop with Jackie and her friend. Making our way back to Jose's, things didn't change there and I felt really sad for her whatever was the matter was very deep seated and I didn't think I would ever see her again after we left. I did write and send Christmas and birthday cards and at first used to get replies though there was nothing long winded about the letters I knew they were ok and still in my world somehow, then they just fizzled out and eventually stopped.

Meanwhile back in Manchester we were undergoing another change in circumstances, our Alex turned up to live with us. I was chuffed to be able to put him up by way of a change. We always got on very well and there was only a four year age gap so we were usually on the same wavelength. He was able to get a job straight away at the local hospital on the switchboard, which meant he also worked shifts like I did. When we were both on the same shifts he slept on a bed settee in the living room, but when we were on opposite shifts we used the nice big double bed as a conveyer belt, as one got out the other got in, it was lovely on winter mornings as the bed was already warmed up. We then started frequenting some of the mainly boys clubs and pubs to keep Alex company so got to know an even bigger circle of friends. We also went to our local pub in Eccles but this presented a problem in itself to me as I always got worried about going to the toilet in a straight pub, no one raised an eyebrow at gay pubs and clubs you were quite likely to get a drag queen or a transvestite in the ladies so wearing a three piece suit and a tie didn't matter, but locally it did dependant on who was in the pub at the time. Anyway you still had to run the gauntlet quite often to someone shouting you're going in the wrong one love, but we got over it and eventually because it was our local people got used to it. It was there that we met a young couple of girls who were going to be our friends for the rest of their lives but unfortunately for them that wasn't a very long time, Angela the feminine girl died during an epileptic fit in hospital and though Dorrie lived longer she was still comparably young when cancer took her from us. But they joined in all our fun and games and I'd like to think they enjoyed their short lives, they certainly enriched ours.

Milly got in touch, it was the one I thought was her girlfriend that rang and we went to meet the in the Union, we had a great night out and started to see a lot of each other whenever they came up from London. Sandy was always with her but they didn't seem very together, I was totally infatuated, she seemed very exotic to me, but I didn't make any definite approaches as I am not into breaking up relationships. It turned out they had been together but the relationship had ended though they still lived together more for convenience than anything else. I checked it out with Sandy myself just to be sure and she gave me her best wishes. I wasn't altogether sure if Milly was interested in me but at least there didn't seem to be anything in the way of me finding out. Well we did get together and relished our times together but of course it was a long distance relationship but where there's a will there's a way.

My mum and Alex celebrated their birthday on the 3rd of October, when he was born his mum had said to my mum I have a very special present for your seventeenth and pulled the covers back and there was our Alex. My mum had been with Aunty Elsie the night before and he didn't look like arriving anytime soon yet there he was the next morning. I am sure that was why we had such a strong bond with him quite apart from us turning out to be gay. We had a very large family so percentage wise I suppose we only had our fair share of gays! Well this year we decided to have a big joint party but to hold it in a club in Manchester, the idea being we wouldn't have to clear up all the mess the next day. We also decided to have it as a fancy dress, I went as an Arab my mum as a Chinese coolie our Alex was a ballet dancer. We had a smashing night all the world and their friends seemed to be there and all too soon closing time was looming. Alex and I ordered black cabs for us as we had some family down and Sandy and Milly were coming back. What happened next was quite funny we all set of home in these cabs, I thought mum was with Alex, he thought she was with me and when we arrived home there was a convoy of black cabs coming up the street apparently the party was going to continue at home. None of them had mum in with them so we rang the club and one of the managers went to look for her, a big order of drinks was on the bar and she thought it was one of our rounds and we'd left it so she downed the lot then wandered out of the club looking for us! The manager of club found her wandering around China town in a very bemused state and eliciting quite a few funny looks in all her fancy dress grandeur, it was lucky no one took offence, anyway she arrived home safely in a cab all of her own. The party went on for days! No one seemed to want to leave there was nearly always someone asleep but it seemed to be like shift work some of them would wake up and start drinking again and so it went on, someone must have gone out and replenished the drinks at some stage but so much for hiring a club to keep the house tidy. When people started going it looked like a shipwreck and what was worse both Alex and myself seemed to have lost our voices. The plan was my mum was going back to London with Milly and when I'd done my shift I would go down on the train and the following week we would all come back together. It was after they had gone that we realised neither of us could go to work as we both needed our voices for the jobs we did him on a switchboard and me on the emergency phone and radio. We went to the doctor and both came out with sick notes one for laryngitis and the other for pharyngitis, what we actually had was alcoholic poisoning, still it got us out of trouble. We went back home got the girl in the flat upstairs to phone our places of work for us then set to cleaning the mess up. The strange thing was we didn't feel at all ill or hung over and we deserved to be it was the 6th of October and the party had started on the 3rd. We made ourselves a nice meal then decided we would just go out to our local for a nice quiet night, of course once we had a few drinks inside us it seemed an even better idea to go to town. We went to the same club as the party had been held at and we were prancing about on the dance floor when who should walk in but Milly and mum. When they set off they had got hopelessly lost so ended going to Milly's mums in Whalley Range. Then deciding they would stay the night and go the next day, they left Sandy at the house as she did have a hangover so the sleep would do her good and she could drive them back the next day. So we had another good night but it seemed funny saying goodnight at the end and Milly and mum going one way whilst we went the other.

So I was to start another chapter of my life with Milly, when my days off fell in midweek I used to travel by train to London and if it was weekend Milly would come to Manchester. It was pretty tiring but if we wanted to see each other that was how it had to be. Sandy was still around all the time and I found that a bit disquieting but they both assured me their relationship was at an end a long time before I appeared on the scene, so I wasn't doing any home breaking. Sandy started having an affair with the landlady of our local pub which was a bit of a surprise I must say, they used to have their dalliances at my flat usually when we were all out, I had a bit of a shock one night when I came home earlier than usual didn't realise they were in and when I went in the bedroom for something apart from being surprised they were there what really threw me was the landlady's beautiful head of hair draped across the bed knob. I hadn't realised it was a wig and it gave me quite a turn I thought she'd been scalped! You didn't see many wigs in those days, but I did come across one earlier in my time in London when I first got there I went home with a girl and when in the middle of our passion I ran my hand through her hair and found myself with a wig in my hand that was a shock but I felt really sorry for the girl as she had a really bad scalp condition so there was only a few tufts of hair here and there.

One of the times I was in London we went to a Chelsea football dinner and dance, a friend of Millys had invited us, it was a very dressy up do and Milly was in a long flowing gown with a mink stole and dripping with jewellery, I had a brand new three piece suit. Afterwards we decided to go to a club, it was all new to me totally different from my Limbo days, these were drinking clubs. Some woman decided to take a dislike to me, I didn't realise why but found out she was an old flame of Milly's. I hadn't even spoken to the woman but as we were leaving to look for a cab she jumped me, before I knew it I was involved in an all out scrap with this woman and a bloke that was with her, I ended up flat on the ground and the bloke kicked me in the head, when I looked up Milly was hanging on his back to stop him doing any more damage and someone else had grabbed the girl. We had to go to hospital as there was blood gushing out of me like a fountain. Whilst we were there we were in separate cubicles and as I was being treated I could hear Milly carrying on about me was I alright etc then there was suddenly silence, I thought perhaps she'd fainted, it turned out they had numbed her lip and put some stitches in it (we found out later the stitches weren't necessary so it was probably to keep her quiet)! In the meantime I was having stitches too in my head and my face bathed with some sort of antiseptic, when we left I looked like the invisible man, my head was swathed in bandages the only bit of my face that was showing was my right eye, nose and mouth. We weren't having much luck flagging a taxi down with me looking like I did so I hid in a doorway till Milly got one. We were in a sorry state when we got home and the pain was starting to manifest itself as the drink and the anaesthetic wore of. So we took painkillers and straight to bed. When we woke up it was still very early but the doorbell was ringing and in no danger of stopping, when we opened it, it was another of Milly's exes who had heard about what happened and came to see if we were ok. I had met this one previously and we got on very well in spite of the fact that Sandy had always been terrified of her and told me to steer clear. Anyway she took one look at us and said is it true that Jean did this, and we said yes with the help of some bloke, right she said and left. The woman had a veg stall at Notting hill gate in the Portabella road market; she used to load up her horse and cart to transfer the produce from where she kept it. I would have loved to see this but was told by numerous people, one that I didn't even meet till years later that Doll (the ex) chased Jean and the horse and cart all the way through the market brandishing a meat cleaver. Obviously she didn't use it but no doubt got her message through, Jean was all sweetness and light and full of apologies next time we saw her. The evening of the day after we went to see Milly's doctor, I actually was afraid I'd lost my eye because of all the bandaging. When he unwound it all I was very pleased I could see despite the two very impressive black eyes I was sporting and seven stitches in my left eyebrow, he bathed it for me and put a plaster on it. When he looked at Milly's lip he started laughing and took the stitches out saying they weren't needed and had she had a lot to say? She had!

Obviously I couldn't go to work looking like a train wreck so I rang and told them I had been involved in an accident. Then we went to Brighton to see some friends of Milly's hopefully ones that didn't want to bash my head in. they didn't they were lovely ladies. I found out two medical things that weekend, the first was that I was allergic to plasters as my face came out in a terrible rash that made me look even worse if that was possible. The other thing was a wonderful new medicine that had just come out in South Africa that the friends knew about because an acquaintance had used it. I was quite often very sick because of my duodenal ulcer, as it happened whilst we were there they told us about it. We got some, had to be specially ordered by the chemist after getting a private prescription from the doctors. I had to be very strict with myself about what when and where to eat for a month and it worked I never had a problem again, some- time later I had an x-ray for something else and it was completely dissipated.

Well time was going on with all the coming and going between Manchester and London we'd come to the conclusion we wanted to be together so something had to be done. I didn't want to just walk out of my job as I'd done in the past (see I was growing up a bit) so set about enquiring if a transfer was possible. Unfortunately the answer was not at the moment and it didn't sound like it was worth waiting. In Manchester fire brigade at that time the control room was manned by women but in London they had men working there who had retired from active service, as well as women, so not much chance of them leaving to get married or have a baby. I had to widen my net having been in a nice career job I didn't want to go down the road of getting any old thing as a means to an end so I took my time and looked around each time I was in London.

Well the job I applied for wasn't everybody's cup of tea it was a traffic wardens job! I didn't actually drive so hadn't thought through the implications of being disliked in general just for doing my job. When I had the interview I told them I would have to give a months-notice at my current job and they said that would be fine. A short while later they informed me I had the job and they would let me know when to give in my notice as I'd have to start on a training date. They did and I left the fire brigade at the weekend before I was due to start my new career.

Back to London

You may think my mum had been keeping quiet during all these arrangements, she hadn't. Quite a few tantrums had taken place with more threats of possible suicide but she had Milly to contend with this time who was more her age than mine and put her in her place in no uncertain terms.

Just before we were due to leave Milly said if I was going to live with her I'd have to learn to drive, I didn't have a problem with that, I'd always wanted to just knew I couldn't afford a car so hadn't bothered. When we came out of the flat she said go on then have a go! It was an automatic so I didn't have to worry about gear changes or anything too complicated so I got in thinking I was just going to the end of my crescent. How wrong can you be? The traffic lights were on green so just carried on with my right turn and didn't even have to stop as we were straight on to the motorway at the Eccles junction. By then my voice had gone up a couple of octaves as I squeaked "I can't do this!" Anyway I was told I didn't have to change lanes as it was a new engine and in those days you had to run them in and couldn't go faster than 50 miles an hour. I was gravitating towards the line to my right as most learners apparently do so she kept saying keep to the middle and eventually I started managing to keep on an even keel. We had been going about an hour and I was feeling quite proud of myself, I took the opportunity to glance at my passenger and was horrified to see she was fast asleep! I couldn't believe it but the cocky side of my nature said well you must be doing all right. A few miles further on instead of trying not to go towards the white line on the driver's side I was wrestling with the steering wheel to stop us going over the one on the passenger side, I could feel the tendons in my neck straining so knew something was very wrong and was shouting at Milly to wake up. So when she did she didn't seem to know any more than I did and said to pull over into the slip road which wasn't difficult as it seemed to want to go there anyway, what was a little problem was how to brake I hadn't had to do that so far, as I'm writing this I can't believe how stupid I was to be driving in the first place! Well when we did eventually stop and get out it was to discover that we had a blow out in the rear passenger side tyre, no wonder I was struggling to keep the car straight. I went to the emergency phone that was fortunately only a few yards down the slip road and when I explained to the lady in the control room what had happened she said she would send one of their vehicles as it was only a tyre instead of getting the RAC. I thought that was a good result but when I told Milly she seemed a bit perturbed and told me when they came to lean over the front of the windscreen. She was a very voluptuous lady and with her low cut tops and false eyelashes she was quite alluring, anyway she turned all her charms on full beam when the police arrived to change our tyre for us, I don't know how they managed to do it without tripping over their tongues! When it was done they even helped us out of the slip road into the flow of traffic, which was just as well as I'd have probably still been there. It took us nearly six hours to get home what with the 50mile limit and the blow out, I was exhausted when we got back didn't realise how tense I'd been for most of the drive. I'd have been even tenser if I'd have known the reason I was draped over the windscreen was because the road tax was out of date, then I also discovered the insurance was in the same condition and what's more she only had a provisional driving licence! Not ever having owned a car never mind driven one this was all new to me but I swore I wasn't going to drive her car again until I had passed my test.

When the mail arrived the next morning I had a letter from my new employers and was shocked to discover that they were taking away my job offer, with no explanation whatsoever! I was distraught and unable to do anything about it, as it was the weekend. After having taken such care for once in my life to make sure I had a job to go to I now found myself unemployed right at the beginning of my new life? Milly couldn't understand why I was upset as she wasn't short of money and if I'd wanted to I could have stayed at home without a job. I took myself off to the employment exchange and after queuing for a considerable time, I ended up being grilled about why I'd given my job up and so on, the only thing they seemed interested in was whether I was entitled to any money or not! I on the other hand had only gone there as I didn't know the area very well and wanted to be pointed in the direction of some employment. It was all getting a bit fraught and I ended up breaking down into floods of tears, which was really annoying, but my control had gone. The lady took me into a private room and decided to listen to me instead of firing questions at me, when I had related all that had happened to me from being offered the position to being told when to give in my notice she said she wasn't surprised I was so upset and they would take them to tribunal for me. I managed to find a job temping for Hornsey council which was quite interesting but not permanent, I never knew where I'd be working from one day to the next sometimes social services, next day pest control and so on. It wasn't for me, as I like a bit of continuity so I scanned the local papers every day waiting for my dream job to appear. I contemplated going on a computer course (very new at the time) and about the same time applied for a position at the New Zealand High Commission, it sounded a bit posh to me and I couldn't visualise them employing a butch northern lass, (I had decide when I moved to London that I wasn't going to be bullied into dressing to suit them so if they didn't like me in trousers and shirts they could do without me). I had also decide if anyone questioned me about my sexuality they would get a straight answer, I was fed up of living a lie with fifty percent of the people I met or worked with, didn't want to do any flag waving just wanted to be myself.

Well the job interview came before the course started and I was fortunate to get the position, I was over the moon. It was as a switchboard operator on a two-position board, which meant there were three of us working together. The lady that had interviewed me was a small dumpy lady probably only just five foot given I was five foot eight you would think I looked large to her, not the case on the morning I started she took me to the switchboard room to introduce me to the girls and get me started. As I stood in the doorway my heart sunk they were both looking at me as if I'd dropped in from another planet, I thought I must have gone too far with the trousers and waistcoat yet it didn't seem to bother Mrs Makenzie, trust me to find a job with a couple of homophobes I thought. Anyway the lady left me to it and the girls put me through my paces showing me the board, explaining the type of calls, which were mainly international, plus the volume of calls, which was quite heavy as there were thousands every day enquiring about emigration. They seemed to settle down and lose the looks they'd been giving me. After I'd been there a week they told me the reason for their reaction when they saw that I had a sense of humour, Mrs Makenzie had told them she had chosen a "petite little northern lass!" Then to be confronted with five foot eight and about eleven stone of very butch looking womanhood they had been taken aback to say the least! I can understand how she thought it during the interview as there was a desk separating us and I have quite a small head and features, plus I tend to wave my hands around somewhat when I'm talking and they are very slender so I suppose that's what registered in her mind. So everything in the garden was rosy and I was to stay there for the next twelve years so it must have been ok.

Whilst all this was going on I was realising what had only been inklings before. My new partner was a "working girl" the idea that she was in public relations was a little far-fetched but when you have already fallen for someone it's too late to get prudish. She worked from a basement flat on the other side of London so nothing usually impinged on our home life, her main offerings were of domination, so not much actual sex involved. I had to try and put any imaginings and jealousy out of my mind, which was difficult at first but it's amazing how you can adapt to certain circumstances if you need to!

Our life swept by in a whirl of new experiences for me, instead of raving around Soho as I did in my first few years in London I was now dining out at posh restaurants and going to the theatre on a fairly regular basis. Mind you there was the nightclubs as well and quite a lot of my time was whizzing past in an alcoholic haze I was having a ball.

I was being spoilt rotten as well, quite a new experience for me, I had a whole wardrobe of elegant suits, silk ties and numerous pairs of shoes. Most of the shoes crippled me so I had to tell her to stop wandering in with them. I was also getting a nice collection of jewellery. I didn't completely feel comfortable with all this knowing where the money was coming from but I made it my business to pay all the household bills, fortunately the flat was a controlled rent so not horrendous London prices.

I arranged to have driving lessons once I was settled in my job. I went with BSM (British school of motoring); it was located in Leicester Square, which was a two-minute walk from work. When I went to my first lesson I was gob smacked when he made me get in and start my lesson there, in my innocence I thought he would have driven me to a less busy place. Anyway I took to it like a duck to water, maybe it was the six-hour drive from Manchester that helped, and my instructor was impressed with me. At the time there was a waiting list of about four months to get your test, he said I was doing so well and I didn't need any more lessons it would be sensible to try and get the test brought forward. So on my next lesson we drove over to Hammersmith to the place they were booked and he patted me on the head and sent me in to tell a pack of lies to the powers that be. He had told me what to say, just as well as I've never been very good at lying, so there I was telling them I had a chance to emigrate and a job offer in the pipeline but it all depended on me having a driving license, It worked and my test was arranged for the following week in Morden, in that case a little dishonestly went a long way.

So my last lesson was to be in Morden to get used to the area and what a good job we went for a trial run, it was totally different from any areas we'd been to before. Lots of quite narrow streets and loads of double-parking so I had a rapid lesson on who had the right of way in that situation. My test was the following week and I was feeling pretty nervous but did amazingly well and passed with flying colours even though I had a disagreement with the instructor about roundabouts! It was in the verbal part of the test and he said I was wrong and I was quite convinced I was right so as soon as I got back to my instructor I asked him the same question I'd been asked and he gave the same answer as me so I wanted him to go back and tell the inspector but he wouldn't let me. My point of view was if someone had more than one mistake and that was one of them it could make the difference between passing and failing. Anyway that was the end of that and I went home feeling very proud. Milly said maybe she would have another go now I'd passed, It was to be her twenty-first attempt, her failures had always been on the verbal part (she was a really good driver), so I went through the highway code with her over and over till she could nearly recite the whole thing from memory and she passed with no problems when she went back so we were legal at last.

The first day after my test she left the car with me and took a taxi to work so I could have a practice without L plates We had a Yorkshire terrier called Suzy Poo, so I thought I'd take her to Primrose hill for her walk, It wasn't far away as we lived in Mornington Crescent, fortunately there were loads of parking spaces as everyone was at worked so I could just pull up and get out. We had a lovely hour in the park and set of home. That's when my troubles started; we lived on a one-way street that was very busy as we were alongside Euston station so lots of traffic used us as a cut through. There was a space outside the house unfortunately in those days parking wasn't included in your lessons. I was forwards and backwards trying to get in this space that started to look smaller every attempt I made. Cars were racing past and I was getting more and more worked up. If I drove round the block one I did it a dozen times and it never looked any better. There was a little triumph parked next door one of the times when I was seesawing back and forth I managed to get our bumpers entwined, fortunately the triumph's bumper was quite pliable rubber and I was able to unhook it cringing every time a car zoomed past, the neighbour was peeping out through her net curtain probably feeling very anxious about this red-faced maniac who was trying to park, why she didn't come out and help I'll never know. We had parking permits so it wasn't like I could drive off and dump the car somewhere else. HOURS later with the dog and myself both cross legged Milly turned up in a taxi "hello darling, have you had a lovely time?" I all but threw the keys at her for her to park up for me; she did it in seconds so smoothly without any problems and couldn't understand why, I was traumatized. I never did learn to park properly till years later when I got a car with power steering.

We went on our first holiday together to Amsterdam, my mum and Cousin Alex came with us. I was still uncomfortable about flying but my mum was petrified and so was Alex so being brave for them took my mind off my own fears, it was only about an hour's flight anyway.

We had a very exhausting week as we were burning the candle at both ends, trying to do all the tourist stuff in the daytime, which was fine but the nightlife there didn't start till very late. The first couple of nights we set off in the early evening and thought it was very quiet everywhere only to find when we were on our way back to the hotel when everyone else was just starting their night's entertainment. We sorted it out in the end but it made for some very bleary –eyed sightseeing trips.

One night Milly and I had out first proper row, drink had a lot to do with it but it was a rip roaring one which culminated in her marching off in one direction and me after slinging her shoes after her and going in the opposite direction. My mum had gone home earlier in a cab and Alex had gone somewhere different. I suddenly realised I hadn't a clue where I was or where I was heading for, a nice young man asked if I was alright and I told him I was lost, he spoke very good English and said he would help me. As we were walking along with me spilling out all my argument to him someone ran up and pushed my shoulder as I turned to see who it was he ran off but so had my nice young man with my wallet in his possession, I felt a right idiot, your warned about that sort of thing but never expect it to happen to you. When I had a proper look at my surroundings I realised I must be in the "red light district", there were bouncers outside strip joints and females for sale in windows displaying their wares. I would have been quite happy with my surroundings in London's Soho but in the middle of the night in a foreign country and penniless I wasn't very happy. I turned round and retraced my steps in the hope I could find my way back to the club we had been in as Alex had been going in as we left and I was hoping he would still be there. Fortunately I bumped into a respectable looking couple who after much waving of arms and gesturing pointed me in the direction of the club. I was so relieved when I saw Alex was still in there that I broke down with my tail of woe. We went back to the hotel to make sure Milly had got back alright .Yan the night porter let us in and said " little mudder home all right, beautiful brown lady home with no shoes, and he'd seen them up to their rooms", so he opened up the bar for us and the three of us had an impromptu party. We staggered off to our rooms at about 5-30am only to be woken up at 6-30 am to get ready for our trip on the canal boats! Milly had forgotten about the row and couldn't remember much about getting back as she'd wandered into another bar on the way back and ended up smoking pot with a group of hippy types, she didn't normally smoke anything so she was well away on her return. When I was telling her about being robbed I suddenly realised the key to the wardrobe was in my wallet as well so we couldn't get our clothes out. We managed to get hold of one of the cleaners and took ages trying to explain as each time we said wardrobe the thought we were talking about the bathroom. All was right in the end and we set off for our trip, feeling much the worse for wear and a wallet and pair of shoes out of pocket. Whoever found the shoes would have felt like they discovered a gold mine as at the time the shoes in Holland were very expensive and the ones we'd lost were brand new, that's why I was carrying them as they had been pinching her feet.

One of the days all of us except Alex went for a mooch round the shops, we went in one and much to my horror when I looked round I was slap bang in the middle of a sex shop! Milly and my mum had shot into a booth and I was left standing in the middle of a whole range of dildo's and whips and suchlike feeling extremely embarrassed and stupid. My eyes fell on an innocent looking tea towel so I picked it up to keep my eyes occupied only to find out it was a cartoon of snow white and the seven dwarfs doing unspeakable things to each other, I dropped that pretty quickly and went to touch a Santa Claus toy, as soon as my hand touched it his cloak opened and a great big willy poked out. When they came out of the booth they were in stitches, partly at what they'd been watching but mainly at me standing ramrod straight in the middle of the shop with a bright red face. It wasn't that I was innocent just that I'd never seen anything like that before, it was pre-Ann Summers shops and there was a man behind the counter which made it worse. The next day the evil duo took our Alex to the same shop and shoved him in the booth they expected him to come running out as it was straight sex films showing and they knew it would embarrass him, he didn't come out but when they looked his feet were sticking out as he had his back to the screen, they had half curtains so you couldn't do anything rude in there. Again they were in hysterics at someone else's expense. I thoroughly checked my baggage before we left the hotel just in case some of the shops merchandise had found its way in there!

When we set of to come back there was very high security at the airport, the police all had high-powered rifles, which was a bit scary. On the way through we had to go in little booths to have our hand luggage searched before moving on to the departure lounge. As we came out we we're chatting and laughing and just moving along with the queue not taking a lot of notice, so we hadn't seen that there were two different queue's one for women the other for men, of course Alex was in the wrong one and the reason for the queue was to have a body frisk, they thought he was being disrespectful expecting a woman to frisk him so when he moved across to the male frisker he was not very gentle about it, or to use our Alex words "he nearly pulled my knackers off". So that was us in giggles again.

Most of our life went along in a fairly sedate fashion given the two of us had totally different lifestyles as far as employment was concerned. We did socialise a lot and unfortunately most of it was on weeknights so from my point of view a bit on the tiring side as I always had to be up early for work, Milly could suit herself what time she went and finished, there isn't a lot of call for domination at eight in the morning.

One evening we were sitting down to have our dinner and Milly said, "I have to go back to the flat and I need you to come with me", she seemed to be a bit ruffled which was unusual for her, so off we went and on the way she explained what had happened. She had a punter who she had tied up in the bathroom as part of his punishment. Then another had arrived who wanted similar treatment so rather than turn him away and lose money she had tied him up naked in the outside toilet thinking the two wouldn't meet so it didn't matter. Then she went round the corner to a snack bar she used and had a snack before going back and letting the man out of the bathroom. After hanging around for a while she thought it's not very busy I may as well call it a day, completely forgetting about man number two! So there we were chasing across London to release someone who had been tied to an outside toilet in the nude for about four hours! It was freezing cold as well so we were expecting trouble, which is why she took me so I could ring the police if there was. When we got there I kept out of the way in the kitchen while she released him and was amazed to hear him thanking her profusely and insisting she had another fifty pounds. There's nothing so strange as folk and at least it confirmed to me that she really did that sort of work rather than all the other stuff I had been imagining.

Another time a close friend who was also in the same line of business but had a flat with a dungeon in it in Victoria rang looking for Milly thinking she was at home as she couldn't get hold of her at work. She wanted her to cane one of her punters while she pranced around doing whatever was required of her and in Milly's absence asked me if I could assist her, not flipping likely I would have been embarrassed and probably falling about laughing at the same time, she couldn't understand why I wouldn't want to earn a hundred quid without even taking my clothes off. A lot of her customers worked in the Whitehall area and I wouldn't like to be in the position of recognising someone that was supposed to be helping run the country.

Another time we had to do a dash across London for a totally different reason, Milly had a lot of very expensive jewellery; she invested most of her earnings in it, as she couldn't really bank her money. She tended to hide what she wasn't wearing in various places around the flat .On her way to work that day she had taken the living room curtains to a dry cleaners and laundry near her other flat, it was only when she wanted to change her rings around for our night out that she remembered where they were hidden, in the hem of the curtains! We flew across London in the hope they weren't closed yet but had just missed them, there was a sign saying they would be open at six am the next day. We were waiting and fortunately they hadn't been done but were just about to be the next batch, phew! The manager was amazed when she saw thousands of pounds worth of diamond rings coming out of the curtain hem. I had visions of her spending her life checking hems in case someone else was that careless.

One of the pubs we used to frequent was on Lambeth Walk, I was quite taken with going there as I'd heard the song about Lambeth walk often but had never thought I'd be going there to a pub. It was called the French Horn and at the time was run by a couple of gay men who Milly was friendly with. We had some really good nights there and nearly always stayed for as shut in. After being there the first time and having to get the car keys to stop Milly driving home, then stupidly doing it myself which was really frightening as I knew I'd had far too much as well, if we went in the car after that I used to throw the keys in the boot which was self- locking and come back in a cab the next day to pick it up.

The boys went on holiday and another couple managed it originally two girls but one of them had a sex change, I was quite fascinated with it all as Milly had told me quite a lot about them before we met and had said the first time they tried to have sex with the newly acquired penis it started to come off and more surgery had to be done, I don't know how true this was as it's not exactly something you can ask. One night we stayed for a lock in when they were there and what used to happen was we only used the gents, as the light didn't show outside like the ladies toilet did. I was in the loo and heard someone come in and use the urinal I peeped out to see if I could manage to get out without disturbing the person and couldn't believe what I saw, it was the sex change at the urinal but peeing out of the base of the penis, he had it dragged right up to allow for the flow. I thought if that's the best they could do I wouldn't have bothered. I assume things are much improved in this day and age.

In the meantime I was really enjoying my job, it was a very busy switchboard so you didn't get chance to get bored. There was quite a good social life there as well; we used to have social gatherings at least once a month in the penthouse, which was lovely. Once we had a charity event in the ballroom, a woolshed dance, a bit like us having a barn dance only there were great bales of wool for us to sit on instead of seats. We had The All Blacks serving as our waiters and bar staff as part of the charity they must have been touring at the time, which was very convenient. We had an auction in which Milly kept sticking her hand up and became the owner of a rugby ball signed by the whole team, she had bid about three hundred pounds for it and promptly gave it back to be re auctioned, I was worried sick that she didn't have that much money on her but she did which was a relief. If she had kept it, it would have probably been worth a lot more in time to come.

When I hadn't been living in London that long my mum was told she could have a council house, I had put my name down when I first went to Eccles so it had come through at last albeit for my mum not me. It was the best thing that could have happened as once she was moved in she settled and didn't have any mad urges to follow me again. Besides we went to visit regularly about once a fortnight as Milly went to her mum's and me to mine. Mum also came to stop with us for a week every now and then which she enjoyed thoroughly as she got spoilt rotten One day we had been for a drink in the afternoon which wasn't usual, when we got back my mum was still in party mode so Milly said get a bottle of wine out, I have never been a wine drinker and didn't know one from the other so asked which one she said it didn't matter so I just grabbed the nearest to hand, my mum was drinking it like water so when I found out it was a two hundred pound bottle she just quaffed I nearly had a fit!

Milly had a sister who was gay as well and her and her partner used to come and stay with us and we had some great times together, going to Brighton quite often. They also came out with us in Manchester when we had a night out or a party, I thought it was great at the time but it was going to be my downfall later on.

We had another holiday this time in Spain it was at the opening of a new resort and you could either have three weeks for the price of two or take a third person free, so of course we took mum. The place was lovely, we had a beautiful apartment, but because it was a special opening our food was included as well so no need to use the lovely kitchen. You had to go up quite a few flights of marble steps to the dining room, bar and ballroom as our apartment was nearly on the beach. On the first night we all had much too much to drink as we had been given sangria at the welcome meeting and liked it so much we had it with our meal as well so by the time we landed in the bar we were well away to

126

oblivion. Milly gave in first and went home as she had nearly fallen and didn't think anyone would be able to lift her if she went down properly, I thought I'd better stay with mum but gave in not long after Milly, couldn't persuade mum to come back as she was having a laugh with a group of Scottish ladies we'd made friends with. So off I toddled to my bed. In the early hours I got up to go to the loo and couldn't believe what I was confronted with, my mum was spark out on the bed settee fully dressed and covered in blood from a busted nose, she had also been sick. We managed to get her cleaned up and undressed, put her in the other bed all without as much as a grunt from her. In the morning we still couldn't wake her up and we'd booked for a trip out. I was fuming at her getting in such a state and had visions of her ruining the holiday. We went on the trip without her. When we got back about five hours later she still hadn't moved so we started to get a bit worried and decided a nice bath might help. A lot heavier than we expected in her unconscious state and I dropped my end, which unfortunately was the head end! We scraped her up and managed to get her in the bath were she started to come round a bit, the next time I looked in on her she was talking to the shower handle as if it was a phone, she was reporting us to the management for putting her in a bath when she didn't want one! It was funny but we decided she was suffering from concussion not just from us dropping her but whatever happened to get her in the state she was in, she looked like she'd gone ten rounds in a boxing ring with a heavy weight, her nose was swollen and her eyes were on the way to being black. When she had a coffee and came round a bit she remembered slipping at the top of one of the flights of marble steps and coming round at the bottom some time later. Her back was very painful and badly bruised so we got hold of one of the couriers and she managed to get some fantastic cream from the pharmacy in the village and it worked like magic she was up and about after a couple of days. Meanwhile all the Scottish ladies were asking about her and sending her messages, she'd obviously made an impression on them as well as on her back.

The first time she came out there was a fancy dress party, hers was easy, we padded her leg up in a bolster case and made a crutch of the sweeping brush, put her arm in a sling and bandaged her head, her black eyes were made a bit worse with the help of some makeup and we made a sign for on her back saying "The wreck of the Esperess". When we walked into the bar their faces were a picture and they were saying, "you poor wee soul, we didn't know you were that bad", then she turned round and showed them the sign. We had another hilarious night and guess who won first prize? Another bottle of champagne, which we talked her in to taking back with us for another time.

During the course of our holiday we were befriended by some of the local chaps, one had an orange grove the others were fishermen. We used to come out of our apartment some days to be confronted with a big basket of oranges or a bowl of fresh fish. We had to thank them but tell them not to bring anymore our kitchen was looking like a supermarket; we gave most of it to our cleaners who really appreciated it.

My life went along in a happy manner, I loved my job and enjoyed my life and thought everything was going to be forever. My life seemed full and happy, even my mum had settled down and was behaving herself, I don't know what she would have been like if we hadn't seen her as often but you have to be thankful for small mercies. Millys mum was a foster parent so Christmas used to be quite exciting as we never knew who would be there or how many so we took sack loads of presents up for all ages and each sex. One time leading up to Christmas Milly had set off buying things for my mum that she thought she would like, she had obviously been carried away as when it came to loading them into the car there were masses of them. Anyway we were with my mum on Christmas eve and of course lots of merry making had taken place, so when it came to bedtime my mum was well away and thought because it was after midnight she should have her presents, we tried to give he just one so that there'd be some to open the next day and knowing how many there was thought it would be quite nice to get some sleep ourselves. In the end we took the least line of resistance and let her have them all, she was thrilled to bits at the amount as well as the quality we even had a few tears so thought perhaps it was worthwhile staying up the extras hour or so.

The next morning she was stomping about like a bear with a sore head which we just put down to a hangover until she said "I'm glad you're enjoying exchanging your presents, but what about me?" She had completely forgotten about the whole carry on we did with her gifts, when I dragged them all from under her bed where we had pushed them she was very shamefaced. After that it became a joke with my mum she was only allowed one present before bedtime, which I was still doing till her very last Christmas.

As time went on Milly's sister and her partner still came to stay but her sister had an illness that precluded her from joining in a lot of what was going on but she still loved being there, she very rarely managed to come out with us for the evening so it was usually just the three of us. I did notice that Milly seemed to be paying more attention to her sisters partner but just put it down as concern that she might get fed up if they couldn't come out as a couple and was trying to fill the gap. One of the times they visited coincided with my mums visit, it was a bit cramped but we managed. As usual we all went out and the sister stayed in, it turned out to be quite a long night and we'd ended up in a club. My mum said she was ready for home so when I asked Milly if she was she said no they'd stop a bit longer. I didn't mind as I had work in the morning so we went and ordered a cab and after waiting about ten minutes realised I hadn't got the door key so popped back in to get it. As I went round the corner it was to see them in a passionate clinch on the dance floor snogging the face of each other! I felt as if someone had hit me in the stomach and I could have been sick, I couldn't actually believe what I was seeing. I just turned around and went home and managed to get in by waking the guy on the ground floor up. My mum went to sleep in her bed in the kitchen (spare bed), and I just sat and waited for them to come home getting more upset as the minutes went by. When they came in I confronted them with it and they at first denied it. Eventually I said that I'd been back in the club and seen them so it was a waste of time lying, just at that stage the sister had heard the raised voices and came out to see what the fuss was and had heard the tail end of what was being said, she didn't believe it and all of a sudden there was an almighty hubbub and I found myself being beaten to a pulp by all three of them. I was so hurt I couldn't even defend myself; I couldn't actually believe what was happening. My mum came in and started to try and drag them off me and somehow I managed to get out of the house. I was heartbroken and in a state of shock as I was reeling around in shock and pain I managed to get a black cab to stop and went to my cousins who fortunately for me had moved back to London.

He couldn't believe the state of me when I knocked him out of bed, black eyes busted nose, and my breasts were purple looked more like I had aubergines strapped to my chest. When I woke up the next day it felt as if it had all been a terrible nightmare, I couldn't believe the betrayal not just by the person who was supposed to love me but even her sister who had also been betrayed had jumped on the bandwagon and helped to beat me up. She was to find the truth of it in time to come when she was deserted and her partner moved in with Milly. I found no pleasure in her comeuppance, as I didn't want anyone to feel the way I did.

I managed to sort out my mums return to Manchester then went to complete another era in my life. When I went to pick up my belongings it was as if I was talking to a complete stranger not the person I had just spent four years of my life with.

What's Next?

I moved in with Alex once again to lick my wounds and try to get back to my version of normal. By this time Alex was with another partner who also did drag shows. Guaranteed to take your mind of things somewhat when you're living amongst big flouncy dresses and wigs. Not to mention the rehearsals of the numbers to get the miming perfect. At first there was just the three of us as the third flat sharer was having a little spell in prison so I was able to use his room. It was none other than Jackie the young man who had introduced me to Cindy when I was an innocent about what was to become my life style.

It's a good job I had my work to keep me steady at the time as I felt like I was going off the rails. My work mates were very supportive when they got over the shock, they knew Milly and they were nearly as surprised as I was by events.

I went out with the boys a lot to do the drag shows, they didn't have a car so when we were going to shows on buses with all the gear we caused quite a stir, some of us with the sequined and frilly frocks others with a couple of polystyrene heads with beautifully coiffed wigs on them. It was great fun and when we weren't doing a show we would go and watch other shows, as you had to keep up with the competition of which there was a lot in those days. This was going some way to cover up my hurt but it didn't make it stop when I had my quiet moments.

Shortly after Jackie returned home but refused to take his room back and said he would manage on the couch. It was really nice of him but I felt like a cuckoo in the nest so set about in a concerted effort to find somewhere new to live. The other thing that spurred me on was he had gone back to his wicked ways and when

I got up some mornings the living room looked like a treasure cave, full of stolen goods! I was frightened to death that we would be raided and I'd end up in prison for receiving. He always managed to bring back a liqueur that I liked and I had a lovely array of after shaves, definitely not worth going to prison for.

I found a bed-sitter in Streatham, it was a bay windowed room so quite large on the first floor plus a decent sized galley kitchen so it was quite an improvement on some of the places I'd had in the past in London's bed-sit land. I had also got over having to live close to my job it seems as it took me an hour and half to get to work but I always made sure I had a good book with me to pass the time.

There were eight bed-sits in the house all rented by girls, yes you'd think I would have been in heaven but at the time I was totally off women and romance. Hard reality had set in once I was settled and it dawned on me I really was on my own again. I just concentrated on my work, didn't even want to go out anywhere, going out with the boys had just been a convenient crutch at the time. The most contact I had with the girls in the house was a good morning or evening, I did wonder if they were concerned at having a lesbian in their midst but didn't worry about it in the least.

Around this time pop, my nana's husband became really ill and I was up and down to Fleetwood quite a bit and when I couldn't manage to go kept in touch by phone, which was easy considering I worked on a switchboard. At about the same time the phone in the house, which was a communal one in the hall was cut off, I never understood why as it was a pay phone so perhaps the landlord had forgotten to pay it, also the emersion heater for the bath was disconnected. I was very concerned that something may happen out of work time and my nana wouldn't be able to get hold of me so was pleased to see one of the girls had put a note in the hallway suggesting we all get together to find out what could be done about the situation. (It wouldn't happen now as everyone has mobile phones).

So we had our meeting and because my room was one of the biggest we had it in there. We sorted out what was to be done about the landlord and who was going to do it and ended up having an impromptu party. Everyone nipped back to their own room and came back bearing a variety of drinks so we all ended up in a very merry state where a lot of true confessions were coming out about things that had happened with different boyfriends, I thought maybe I'd better mention that I was bent in case they would feel odd about it if they found out later. They were all fine and I found myself telling them about my situation and having all shared a few secrets we became friends. (I'm still in touch with two of them thirty-five years later).

I had the inevitable call to say pop was asking to see me, so I went straight away, quite a journey at the time with lots of train changes. They said he perked up when I was there so I was pleased about that but because of work I had to set of back more or less the same day. The phone at home had been put back on and by the time I got back there was a message for me to phone, my heart sunk and I was right he had passed away whilst I was on the way home. He knew he was going and had said he had just wanted to see me before he went, bless him he was a lovely man.

Well having got to know each other because of a crisis in the house, we all found that we got on quite well and often cooked each other meals and had get togethers. It made it nice to come home from work to instead of the silence of a single room and your own thoughts. We obviously all chatted about our trials and tribulations and got to know each other pretty well.

I don't know to this day how they managed it but I came home from work to find my door open and a set of my clothes laid out over the settee, not the kind of clothes I'd ever worn in front of them, one of my three piece suits, matching tie, shirt even shoes. I was still standing there looking bemused when one of the girls came in and said that they had a bath running for me and my dinner was ready in Marion's room! All I had to do was eat the meal have a bath and get myself ready for a night out at one of my gay venues, oh and choose which of the girls I would take with me as my pretend partner! I was really touched by their concern as I'd said I couldn't bring myself to go out in case I was confronted with my ex and her partner, I'd lost a lot of my usual confidence.

That was to start a round of brilliant nights out which boosted my reputation no end, every time I went out I had a different girl with me, the people I bumped into that knew me must have wondered where I was finding them all. They always acted the part of being with me rather than just knowing me.

It was quite amusing one night; we went to a girl's night at the Sols Arms. We hadn't been there long when a butch I'd known from my Limbo days came in. She was very taken with my "date for the night" and was all but drooling. She bought us a drink and went back to the company she was with but kept coming back to us. I'd told Marion that she had an admirer and she thought it was funny but begged me to make sure she wasn't left alone. Eventually the girl came over and asked if she could borrow my partner for a dance? I said it was up to her, well as it was a fast dance she accepted as she liked dancing and I was close to useless as a dancer. There were a couple of fast ones in a row then it suddenly switched to the slowest of slow dances as the evening was drawing to a close, as I looked across I saw the panic struck look on Marion's face as the girl drew her into a clinch. I marched across the dance floor to claim "my woman" back out of her clutches. It was hilarious really as she ended up dancing very closely with me to try and look like the lovers we were supposed to be. We giggled all the way home as she said, "better the devil you know".

Round about this time we had a change of High Commissioner at New Zealand house. He did what I thought was a very nice thing and arranged a series of after work get-togethers so he could meet all his staff individually, from the cleaners to the private secretary's. When it was my evening to go I'd been on the switchboard till six so everyone else had been in there about an hour. Sir Douglas was at the door to greet me as I arrived, I went in and got a drink and as there didn't seem to be any seating I sat on a long table that was there, a little lady came and said "I could do with a sit down but don't think I could get on", I got off and gave her a lift up. So there we were sat swinging our legs and chattering away about nothing in particular, I thought she was a secretary I hadn't met until the supervisor of the typing pool came and said "can I get you another drink Lady Carter", oops that was me well and truly foot in mouth again giving Sir Douglas's wife a boost on to the table. Anyway we got our new drinks and stayed chatting away, she asked me my name and told me hers was Sunny, which suited her down to the ground as she was. I think when her husband came over and saw how well we were getting on he was really pleased. Although they were Sir and Lady Carter they weren't full of airs and graces, they were farming stock and though their farm was probably the size of England nevertheless it was still a farm, so they appreciated my down to earth attitude and it was to be the start of a good working relationship.

When they were familiarising themselves with the building, Lady Carter noticed that some of the toilet seats in the ladies public toilets were cracked. This was to start the saga of the toilet seats; she reported it to building services and left it to them to sort it out. What she didn't realise was these particular toilet seats were provided by a company that was no longer in existence, so building services took it upon themselves to go round all the staff toilets and exchange bad for good. I wasn't a bit impressed with this as there were only three of us using the toilets on our floor and they had been replaced with two grotty cracked ones that pinched your bottom when you sat on it. I put a complaint in but nothing was done about it. I was on a little committee that had been formed under the new management and we had fairly informal meetings once a month with Sir Douglas where we were given a glass of wine or two and asked to air our views about anything that was affecting the staff in any way. There wasn't usually many complaints but his face was a picture when I set off about my toilet seat, he couldn't understand how we'd gone from having perfectly good ones to second hand ones. I explained that his wife had asked for new ones in the public area and that's how it happened, she was actually in the kitchen part of the room we was in so he asked her, when she found out what had happened she was amazed that they hadn't bought new and said they would make sure it was rectified. So I suppose building services got a flea in their ear but perhaps explained that the type we had wasn't available any more. Weeks went by and still no sign of new toilet seats, when I talked to building services they were very polite but ignored me just the same. I decided to write a poem about it, which I stuck, on Sir Douglas's office door. The next day he came to the switch room himself took me by the hand and took me to the toilet to show him the offending article! He got down on his knees measured it and said he would go and find one for me himself. I must say we ended up with the poshest toilet seat of the building as he went and got it from Harrods! I've never set foot in there but I did spend many a penny on a Harrods toilet seat. I don't know what happened to everyone else but I was happy with my results. If you don't ask you don't get.

Another thing that I managed to change was our Christmas bottle, every year we were given a litre bottle of spirits as a gift, which was lovely but they always gave the ladies gin and the men whisky. I've never been able to stand gin so always ended up giving mine away. After I had a word they told us all to let them know what we preferred and everyone was happy, strange thing was it turned out that the men seemed to prefer the gin, anyway a satisfactory outcome.

I think Sir and Lady Carter were quite tickled with me as I always said it like it was. They used to have quite a lot of dignitary's visiting and held cocktail evenings for them, funny thing was I was invited to all of them, I think I was there to keep them amused as there wasn't any deep conversations taking place we all just used to have fun. I quite often took one of them out with me to a gay pub or a party and they used to enjoy it. We used to have a code room where sensitive or secret stuff used to happen, every now and then I'd get a message via there from one of the dignitary's I'd entertained, this was all over a matter of time of course.

Back at the bed-sits we were all getting on famously, we discovered that most of us enjoyed swimming. As luck would have it there was a great open-air lido on Tooting common which was only a ten-minute walk from us so we used to go quite regularly. When we first started going we noticed a few furtive looking characters lurking around the common but took no notice, until I suddenly kept getting approached by them asking for sex! What I couldn't understand was why ask me when there were usually three or four of us and all the others were very pretty feminine girls. We found out quite by chance when we mentioned it in a local pub, it turned out the path we were taking was a pick up point for punters to get prostitutes and the signal that they were available was a plastic carrier bag! I thought it was hilarious but nevertheless stopped putting my swimming gear in a carrier.

On one of the nights out to the Sols Arms I met up with two people from my past, who had ended up together. One of them was Cass who was one of the girls that came to live in Fleetwood whilst I was still in the army; the other was a girl I'd met in Soho when I first went to London. At the time she was very keen on a friend of mine and when she'd finished her nights work as a stripper she used to take my friend to breakfast. I never knew if anything else developed but my friend really enjoyed her food so who knows!

It really is a small world and on the gay scene, especially then you would find paths crossing. Not long after our reunion they split up and I ended up being a shoulder to cry on for Pat, unfortunately it got a bit out of hand and she developed a crush on me, which I didn't realise at first. She used to drive round in a huge camper van so if she didn't get home she wasn't worried and would just park up somewhere and sleep there till the next day. On a few occasions she ferried people to parties, I cringe when I think about it now as most of the time she must have been well over the limit with alcohol. So one night she gave me a lift home as Streatham was off the beaten track as far as tubes were concerned and the night buses were few and far between. Of course I invited her in for a drink and that's when the fun and games began, she decided to give me an impromptu strip show in memory of what used to be. Well in the first place I had never seen her do it originally and if I had the difference had to be about six stone! She used to be a dainty little thing and there was this baby elephant prancing around my bed-sit nearly in time to my favourite Barry White record. I didn't know where to look; it was so embarrassing, especially as she thought she was so wonderful and sexy. It was supposed to be a big turn on but I couldn't get her out of the house quick enough whilst still trying not to hurt her feelings. Anyway that was that I thought.

Round about this time I went to the White Bear in Kennington with one of my bed-sit escorts, it was nice there as sometimes they had singers and other times a drag queen. It had a round shaped bar so you could see across the room whichever side you stood. This particular night I became aware of someone looking at me from across the room, all I could see was a face surrounded by a halo of white fur and couldn't be sure but thought I was being winked at. I did a quick check to make sure no-one was standing behind me and came to the conclusion that it was directed at me. How do you casually get from one side of the room to the other and look like you arrived there by accident? Pretty impossible so all that was left was the direct approach, so my escort and I went across and introduced ourselves. There was three people there Maggie (the one that winked), Julie and Betty. It turned out I knew Betty from the Union in Manchester as she used to wait on there on special occasions. I had seen her there one New Year's Eve all done up in her family's tartan, she was a very butch lady so I reckon that's the only time anyone would have seen her legs, well in public anyway. A pleasant evening passed by and lots of swapping of phone numbers ensued with promises to ring.

I did like her but wasn't at all sure what the relationships where between the three of them so didn't pursue it any further, having been on the end of a broken relationship because of someone else horning in I thought I'd leave well enough alone.

Fate Intervenes

Things carried on in the same manner for a while, having great nights out with my lovely bed-sit girls, who were quite enjoying the different experiences and meeting people with a different way of life. They also took it in turns to come to the social evenings at work which were always fun. Sometimes themed so a bit of fancy dress was involved, always fun with ample amounts of extra strong duty free booze available.

I decided to go for a bit of a break to Manchester and see my mum. We would also take a couple of days and go by coach to see my nana. That was the only time I missed having a car, I hated driving in London but would have sooner been zipping along the motorway in a car than coach or train travel

One of our nights out in Manchester who should we bump into but the lady with the sneaky wink. She was there to visit Betty who we then found out was her ex-partner, she also said that Julie and her had been together but they weren't any longer though still remained friends and lived across from each other on the same estate. We all had a pleasant evening together and parted company promising we would phone this time. The only reason I hadn't was because I thought she was with someone and didn't want to step on any ones toes. My mum thought she was very nice and was trying to encourage me to make a date but I wasn't sure about going for another relationship after the horrible ending of the last one. I also think I was enjoying squiring my straight mates around that I wasn't really missing being involved with anyone.

Eventually we did get in touch and arranged to meet in another pub that was on Lambeth walk. It was Easter weekend and she said she was singing a solo at the church in the morning but they would all come to the pub after if I wanted to join them. They were Julie, Betty, Maggie and another friend who wasn't gay, I took one of my pals with me for back up so it wasn't exactly a date but a gathering so no pressure. It turned out to be quite funny as the girl who had taken a shine to me and did the impromptu strip was there and her sister was the afternoons entertainment which also turned out to be a strip act, must say they were like chalk and cheese size wise the sister was like a whittled down clothes prop! I got a bit of a telling off from the landlord for taking pictures of the act, I didn't realise you wasn't allowed to. When it was developed you couldn't see who it was anyway too far away. One of the other pictures was of me, Maggie and her two exes (I wasn't all together sure that Julie was an ex) so I named the photo past, present and future, I suppose that was a bit cocky but I was starting to feel brave again.

We met up a few times always with other people in tow and had a few getting to know each other phone calls. We seemed to be in the same pub as a rule but we had decided to have a proper date in a club. The night we were arranging it my (stalker) turned up and I had told Maggie all about it and decided to try and sneak out while she wasn't looking as I had a bus to catch.

The next night we met up at the pub to go to the club and Maggie was on crutches! Apparently when I left Pat had started to follow me out and Maggie had made a run for the door to try and warn me, outside she tripped over an uneven paving slab and broke her leg, you could say she fell for me. Unfortunately she was supposed to have had a driving test that day and of course had to cancel it, she never did take it again. Anyway we went off to the club but it wasn't exactly a successful night as it was a disco, that didn't go very well with the crutches. We managed to have the last dance which of course was slow so we literally shuffled around with me taking the place of the crutches, at least she never found out how bad my dancing was.

A few nights later I'd been out for the evening and just after I got in the doorbell went, I looked out of the window and there was Pats camper van on my front, I grabbed Marion and told her and she said she would go in my room and pretend to be someone else with me in case she managed to get in. I had to answer the door else someone else would have and she was waking everyone in the house up as it was. I tried to get rid of her nicely but she was drunk and not having it, she was swearing undying love and saying how she needed me, I couldn't credit it I didn't carry one like that when I was dumped by someone I'd spent four years of my life with and been in love with. She was obviously living in a fantasy world, as I hadn't had anything to do with her other than being a shoulder to cry on and witnessing her horrible strip show. She was pushing her way in and there was nothing very dainty about her, whilst I was trying to push her out Marion was leaning over the banister saying " hurry up darling I'm waiting for you" which we thought was hysterical after the event but didn't do much to help at the time. By now she was getting violent and threatening to do allsorts to me and herself, in the tussle she fell forward and somehow her nose connected with my knee and on top of everything else we had blood spurting all over from her nose. Somehow I managed to get her out of the door and shut it, by then all the girls in the house were awake not to mention half of Pendle Avenue. She wouldn't shut up or go away and in the end I had to ring the police. I don't know what they thought, probably assumed it was a lovers tiff, rather than take her away they put her in the camper van, relieved her of her keys and somehow secured it so she couldn't get out. They came and gave her keys back to her in the early morning and sent her off on her way. What a performance, I'd like to say that was the end of it but she seemed to manage to turn up wherever I went for quite a while until she realised I really wasn't interested, phew!

In the meantime my relationship with Maggie had gone no further than dating. My mum came down for a long weekend and we were invited for a meal at Maggie's home, it was to be my first visit so didn't quite know what to expect. The meal was very nice duck a la orange; I'd never had it and quite enjoyed it (what I didn't know was Julie was the one who had done the cooking and then Cinderella like had gone home before we arrived). After the meal we went out to the Elephant and Castle pub and Julie came as well. There was a live band on and Julie said Maggie used to get up and do a couple of songs as a rule. Of course we encouraged her to get up but she was a bit reluctant as it wasn't the usual pianist. Anyway she did in the end and they couldn't get the right key for her so she was mortified and came down, I never ever heard her sing the whole time I knew her because of that, yet the people at her church said she had a great voice. Just shows it doesn't take much to break your confidence.

So a little time went by and I thought we should be taking things a bit further, but Julie always seemed to be there and though they both assured me they were no longer together I still felt uncomfortable about it. One night we decided to go back to mine early, and said goodbye to Julie and left her in the pub. We were well in to what we had gone home to do when the flat door burst open and a very distraught Julie came in! To say it was a dampener was an understatement, they had words and eventually Julie went back home in a taxi, which we provided the money for. This wasn't looking like a very good start to our relationship and some explaining was required.

Apparently they had known each other since they were children and were brought up in an orphanage in Box Hill. Maggie was a year older and left first to become nurse as you got to live in nurse's quarters. Anyway she met a chap and they got engaged but as she was a ward of court because of what happened to her as a child she had to get permission to get married, this was denied as she was too young in their opinion. So the usual occurred she became pregnant and they let her get married. When Julie was old enough to leave the orphanage she gravitated to where her best friend was living. This isn't really to do with my story except in the way it would interfere with things later on. It was a lot more convoluted than that, but long story short they ended up having a relationship which was very on and off and carried on in that vein for most of their lives. Maggie had two teenage girls from her marriage and a three-year-old son who wasn't and Julie had a teenage son slightly younger than the girls. The three teenagers had been partially brought up together so looked on each other as brother and sisters. So I could see if I entered into this relationship there was going to be a fair amount of baggage. Very early days but your head doesn't often get involved where the hearts concerned.

Another New Era

I think it was my thirty-fifth birthday that year, the only way I've come to that conclusion is the Pope was visiting London and I'm pretty sure it was nineteen eighty one, if I'm wrong about that then it was a different birthday I was celebrating, it was just a bench mark as we were going out by then. Maggie had arranged a bit of a party in the pub we had been frequenting on Lambeth walk. It was a nice surprise as I'd never had anything like that before, beautiful red roses were passed over the bar and champagne for everyone. I didn't actually like champagne but the landlady put brandy in it and it was lovely.

We weren't living together at this stage so quite a lot of my time was spent going to and fro from Streatham to Bermondsey, that's what made me remember the pope visiting the day he was actually in London it took me over three hours to get to Bermondsey.

As time went on I discovered she was in quite a bit of debt with her rent, gas and electricity bills. It amounted to nearly thirteen hundred pounds, a lot of money in those days. I wasn't judgemental about it, I'd been brought up surrounded by debt a lot of the time but it frightened me to have something like that hanging over us. At the time I paid fifty pounds a month for my rent, so I went to the bank and asked would I be able to take out a loan for "home improvements". I'd never had a bank loan so was amazed when they said I could have a loan for fifteen hundred pounds and pay it back at fifty four pounds a month. So I went off and discussed it with Maggie saying a solution was to move in with her and pay the loan with what would have been my rent money. She didn't want me to pay the debt but to me it seemed a reasonable thing to do if you were with someone you wanted everything to be as smooth as possible. So that was sorted and with the spare two hundred pounds we went on holiday to visit my nana with the youngest daughter and the three-year old boy. If only I'd had the gift of foresight!

The boys dad used to say he was coming to see him and get him all excited and then not come till after his bed- time. I was annoyed about this, as he obviously wanted to see the mother not the child, though she insisted that there was nothing between them and it had just been a one off incident! She may not have been interested in him but it didn't stop whatever it was he was feeling.

Around the same period the youngest daughter went into hospital to give birth to her little boy, I wasn't allowed in the room with her mum because I wasn't related, they obviously didn't accept same sex partnerships at the time. So you can imagine my outrage when they let her little brother's father in. I bit it down and didn't say anything at the time but I was very hurt.

Not long after Maggie's ex the lady in Manchester became very ill and she was upset and wanted to go and see her, which I understood and didn't mind. Not long after she passed away and Maggie went up and stayed with my mum so she could go to the funeral. Again I understood, but what was really getting me down our relationship, which was still very new, was suffering, as soon as anything intimate was attempted there was much weeping and wailing for her departed friend. I was of the opinion if she thought that much of her she shouldn't have finished with her in the first place.

The straw that broke the camel's back came in the shape of my mum, she came on holiday for a week or so. One of the nights we went to a cheese and wine party at the church hall. All the people there where friends of Maggie and Julie so as far as they were concerned I was the big bad wolf that had broken their relationship! No matter what I said they obviously had Julie's version of events and weren't interested with mine. I didn't like wine and neither did the vicar so we found ourselves a nice little nook and got tucked in to a bottle of whiskey he had brought, he was a really nice chap we got on well. On the way home all of us a little worse for wear but my mum way out in the lead drink wise suddenly kicked off and pushed me to the ground and gave me a thorough kicking, it took Julie and Maggie some time to get her off me. When we got back to the estate they decided to go back to Julies for coffee. I'd had enough of everything and went home, I swallowed a hundred of my mum's sleeping pills and hoped for oblivion (never felt suicidal in my life before having had to cope with my mums shenanigans, but I just wanted out).

As luck would have it Julie came over to get a packet of fags for my mum and found me before it was too late otherwise I wouldn't be sat here writing this. I came round in the hospital three days later so I very nearly succeeded to find a way out from my mounting problems.

I found it hard to believe that I'd felt so desperate that I'd resorted to trying to get rid of myself, mind you I suppose it makes a change that cigarettes saved a life in this instance. Maggie said that she would prefer me to move out, as she didn't want her family exposed to the possibility that I would try it again. I wouldn't I was totally disgusted with myself but I could see her point and said I'd go when I found somewhere.

As luck would have it some months before there had been an advert on the local television news, offering hard to let flats from the council to single people. I had managed to put my name down along with one of the girls from the bed-sit. When I picked my mail up from my old address there was a letter offering us a viewing, unfortunately the other girl had left for a better job elsewhere but Maggie came with me so they assumed she was the second person and I got the flat. I don't know what I was expecting but it was a maisonette and the décor and everything was fine, it was in a seven story flat in Battersea so I assumed it was because it was in a block it was hard to let. Anyway I signed up for it and that was to be the start of three years of poverty for me! The rent was fifty pounds a month and the loan, which I had been paying instead of rent, was fifty-four pounds a month. Where I worked gave us a loan so we could buy an annual travel pass which fortunately was taken out of our wages before we got them, which left me just short of four pounds a week to live off! Thankfully the heating and water rates were included in the rent so I could at least keep warm and clean.

All I had in the furniture department was a single bed, a black and white telly and a settee. Maggie gave me an old double wardrobe, which had to be dismantled and rebuilt, whilst I was doing that I knelt on a rusty nail and ended up in casualty with a very painful infected knee. All in all it was a very depressing period in my life.

I also found out why they were classed as hard to let, it wasn't the property that was the problem but the fact that there'd been a couple of rapes in the lifts that you had to use to get to your home and a murder on the estate. Lovely, the flat was in good nick but would you live long enough to enjoy it? Also they were going to change the address probably in the hope that it would help its reputation. So the first letter I wrote to my mum gave I her the address which was Frances Chichester court and a really high number, I told her not to write it in her address book as it was going to change shortly, she thought I was going to be on the move again and asked me what I was playing at? I thought it was quite funny a little late for her to get all maternal and concerned now! Anyway it was a much more manageable address when it came, 65, Youngs Court. Though the start there was bad I quite enjoyed most of my time there.

The main bonus I discovered was just round the corner on Battersea Park Road was a lovely gay pub that I hadn't known about before, it was called the Cricketers and during the next six years I was to have some wonderful times and make a lot of new friends.

Meanwhile my relationship with Maggie hadn't ceased just stuttered a lot, she seemed a lot more relaxed with me being out of her home and she came over often and usually stayed as long as she could so long as someone was looking after her little boy. My lack of money meant we didn't have much of a social life but at the time it didn't seem to matter, what more could you want in life than a broken down black and white telly and a carpet less floor? At first she offered to pay some of the money back but that resolution didn't hang around for long.

Throughout all this time I'd belonged to a darts team and fortunately for me the landlady of the pub I played for changed premises and the new one was nearer to me so I continued to play just couldn't go mad in the drinks department not having any money, Maggie joined the team as well and turned out to be quite a good player so at least we had that in common to help us along.

We trundled along in this situation and my main goal in life was to get to the end of the three years it would take to repay the loan, I never once defaulted on the payment even though it was a struggle, I hate debt it frightens me but I was proud that I paid it in full. It was probably one of the most stupid things I've ever done (apart from my suicide attempt of course) but when you're looking at things through rose coloured glasses you don't see the dangers. I have always been very loyal and thought I was entering into a forever partnership, I still hadn't learned even after two previous disastrous relationships where I was dumped in no uncertain terms. You have to learn to trust again else your whole life could be a complete misery. Well that statement came back to bite me in the bum often in the next fifteen turbulent years.

As time went on and I was getting towards the end of three years of penny pinching I realised that Maggie was staying for longer periods and more often than not Danny was with her, we were becoming like a little family. I always try and look on the positive side of things so said why not move in seeing as she was at mine more than not. She said she would love to, so I said if she was moving in she had to do it properly and give her flat up, I didn't want her having a ready-made bolt hole for if things were getting sticky, we were either together or not. At first everything was fine. Danny was enrolled into the local school so he was making friends instead of being here one minute and there the next. We used to go to church every Sunday over at the Elephant and Castle, which was a bit of a trek but I didn't want her to lose touch with her friends in the church. After the service was over we used to go to a local pub to meet up with Bert who was Daniels godfather. I wasn't religious but had I been I think I would have been a bit puritanical, it didn't seem right to me to come straight out of church and spend the next four hours or so getting blasted! The other thing I couldn't quite grasp was Bert did all the paying, I used to insist on buying him a drink but everyone else seemed quite happy to let him spend his money, He also used to bring a joint of meat and a huge bag of fruit and vegetables, ostensibly for Maggie and Daniel but she used to give it to Julie, who was always there, at least she had a girlfriend of her own now but still used to try and monopolise Maggie. I expect anyone reading this will think I was pretty stupid the way things were going, I couldn't agree more; hindsight is a wonderful thing!

One of the girls I worked with an Australian lass said she played darts for a good team and why didn't we come and join her them as it was nearer to where I lived. When we went I realised why she'd invited us when she introduced us to her girlfriend. She hadn't wanted anyone at work to find out she was gay which was fair enough. We had some fun times together and often went to their place for Sunday lunch, which usually comprised of nearly every vegetable you could think of and Yorkshire puddings but no meat! Well times were hard so Terry used to put apple sauce, mustard, mint sauce, horse radish and any other condiment that came to hand then all you had to do was imagine your meat and use the appropriate sauce. We had some really great dinners that way; I used to mainly use mint sauce, as lamb was my favourite! Terry was a strange shape, she was five foot ten but only had twenty seven inch inside legs, she was large as well and used to wear collarless granddad shirt that came down to the back of her knees which made her very small legs all but invisible. She used to be a shot putter when she was younger and unfortunately all the muscle she'd built up wasn't muscle anymore.

One of the guys I made friends with in the Cricketers turned out to know my ex Milly from way back he also knew Doll and when we got chatting it turned out he saw Doll the day she chased the woman that beat me up legging it down Portobella Road with her horse and cart. It really is a small world; he and I are still in touch after all this time.

The Not So Little Green Eye

I wasn't normally a jealous person but once bitten twice shy. We made friends with a woman that lived in the area, she was a very nice person but I was sure Maggie was flirting with her. When I confronted her she told me not to be stupid it was all in my mind, I let it go but didn't feel comfortable about it, I took more notice of my surroundings after that and she was definitely doing the sneaky little winks that got me hooked in the first place. I just tried to make sure the opportunity for her to go off the rails didn't arise.

My nana became poorly and I went to Fleetwood to see if I could help out, Maggie didn't come, as it would have meant taking Danny out of school. I was away about a week and when I came back instead of being pleased to see me she was acting very shifty. When I went to give her a hug I could see why, she had love bites all over her neck. I went mad and was quite convinced it was the woman she'd been flirting with, when I did get it out of her it was even worse, it was the barmaid from the Cricketers. I was fuming and stalked out of the house to go and confront her, when I walked in the chap I'd made friends with was sitting there and he took one look at my face and drew me to him for a cuddle, that did it I was breaking my heart and instead of fury there was sorrow. The culprit had rushed off to the other side of the bar when I came in and I saw the futility of making a scene, it took two to tango and no one forced my partner to join the dance.

I forgave her after all her pleas of "I had too much to drink and didn't know what I was doing, it won't happen again". I felt stupid going in the pub and thinking everyone knew but it turned out I had more support than I realised.

Julie went back to Australia for a holiday and whilst she was there she met up with her first love, the flames were rekindled and when she came back she told Terry and gave her notice in at work and went back to Australia for good about a month later. Terry was beside herself with grief over the split and I did everything I could to help her through it, knowing how I'd felt when my previous relationship finished so badly. I was always there if she needed someone to talk to or a shoulder to cry on I'd even took her out to the pub with my last pound when she was feeling particularly down. Eventually with a lot of support she seemed to be levelling out and I was pleased for her.

More Of The Same

Throughout all this period I was still enjoying my job and my friends there did provide a support network when I needed it. There were still all the socials, which meant I wasn't completely bereft of entertainment while I was struggling financially and some of the functions even provided food which was a huge plus when I was struggling to buy food.

One of the commissionaires that worked there used to bring in one of the hottest curries I've ever tasted. When he worked the night shift he used to bring in an extra portion for me and leave it in the switch room for me. I had to save it for when I'd finished work as the first time I made the mistake of having it at lunchtime I discovered my lips went numb and I couldn't feel my tongue, made life difficult on the switchboard no-one could understand a word I was saying. It was delicious though and it provided a much appreciated meal at least one a week.

We plodded on together with some ups and downs as happens with everyone, there always seemed to be a lot of drink involved which led on to quite a few parties some at my home as we were more or less on the doorstep of the pub.

At one of the parties in my home I felt I'd had enough to drink and excused myself and went to bed, leaving everything in full swing, at some stage I got up to us the toilet and as I walked past the stairs what should I see but Maggie in the arms of Terry (who was so heartbroken) nearly devouring each other on the bottom steps of the stairs. I couldn't credit that she could do that to me after all the support I'd given her. To say I was furious would be an understatement, the party was definitely over and as I ushered everyone out feeling really stupid and used I apologised for breaking the night up, I can't believe I managed to be so civil to everyone when I felt more like murdering someone! Anyway when everyone had left a huge row ensued where the pair of them tried to convince me I'd imagined it, as I was half asleep and half sloshed. I saw Terry to the door and told her not to set foot inside it again. As usual I was prepared to let sleeping dogs lie just in case I was mistaken, though I was sure I wasn't but I just couldn't believe how anyone could be so barefaced about it all and act as if nothing had happened.

I had an afternoon off work and came home unexpectedly, no-one home so I went to Terry's and found them together again, only this time I told Maggie to move out and I didn't want anything to do with her anymore. I managed to keep cool throughout the exchange and left them to it. So she went within a couple of days whilst I was at work.

Once more I was completely gutted but I was more hurt at how I'd been treated by my so called friend, I knew Maggie wasn't exactly the faithful sort but expected more from my friend!

I couldn't seem to stay in the house alone so used to come home from work eat, washed and changed and down the pub. I went on a bit of a rampage for a while and didn't want to go home alone so chatted up whoever was available and took them home with me, I thought I was being very noble and up front with them by saying I wasn't looking for a relationship just a one night stand! If I'd been a man saying all that I would have had a few choice words hurled at me, it was like they didn't really believe me so they still came. It wasn't even the sex that I was interested in when I think about it now, I just didn't want to be alone and given I'd just been betrayed yet again I suppose I wanted to know if I was lacking in some way, so needed a boost to my ego. I must say when I got over myself eventually I did feel rather ashamed at the way I'd used those women. Though before I started to feel ashamed I must say I started to enjoy my chauvinistic life style and all it entailed. One Saturday night I went in the Cricketers with a gay lad I was friendly with and whilst we were standing at the bar waiting for our drinks I glanced along the bar and standing together were my Monday to Friday conquests all happily chatting to each other, oops! I could either slink of and go elsewhere or confront the situation. So I walked up to them and said hello, would they like a drink? Then said if they wanted they could sort out between them, which one wanted to come home with me that night and I'd see her at closing time! I fully expected to be wearing the drinks I'd bought them when I turned and walked away, but no, the lucky person was waiting for me at closing time!

I think that's when I realised I had been going too far and was doing no more but using people which I hate, it was just the state of mind I was in at the time. So I put a stop to my womanising and just had parties every night for a while most of which I went to bed in the middle of and left them to it, I suppose I was lucky I wasn't robbed blind but as it was all gay people there I used, to get up in the morning and find my home all clean and tidy as the boys wouldn't leave it in a mess for me to get up to.

Again I was being given a lot of moral support by my workmates, which was nice. I'd been avoiding going to darts as Maggie and Terry were in the team and I wasn't sure how I would cope. My workmates said I should confront the situation as my weekly darts had been a big part of my life and why should I miss it sort of thing, easier said than done. Anyway I rang up and had a word with the team captain and tried to find out if they had been playing, she confirmed they had but no-one had been told that we'd split up and they were together she just thought I had been away or not well from what Maggie had said! I said I'd give it a whirl but wasn't sure if I'd manage or not. When I went I was a bag of nerves and it was difficult to play very well with them together and no-one talking to each other. As the match finished I said goodbye to the rest of the team and headed for home barley keeping the tears at bay. You can imagine my surprise when I found Terry had run after me and was yanking me round threatening to bash my brains out, it was them that had done the dirty on me so I didn't get it! Fortunately the captain and the landlady of the pub had watched her charge out after me and followed, probably saved my bacon as Terry was huge and could have easily pasted me. I was quite shaken when I got home fortunately I hadn't had a drink not knowing what to expect I'd wanted to have my wits about me. The next day the landlady rang to say they had chucked them off the team so not to worry about coming back. I thought it was nice of them to stick up for me. I did start getting some more phone calls that weren't quite so nice from Terry all very threatening and menacing for what reason I didn't know, I had the switchboard listen in to some of them and told her she would be reported to the police if she didn't stop, eventually it did.

It was to be nine months before I saw them again, they had joined another darts team in the same league so when we were due to play at their pub I didn't go it was easier and no-one was made to feel uncomfortable. I did however know exactly what was going on in their lives as Maggie's eldest daughters partner used to come and visit me on a regular basis as he'd had some things from a catalogue I ran. He kept me up to date quite gleefully at some of their arguments and mishaps as he couldn't stand Terry and had a high regard for me. It pleased me that all was not running smoothly after the way I felt I'd been treated, I particularly enjoyed the episode of Maggie crowning Terry with a very heavy log end ashtray, It's a wonder she didn't kill her as it was really heavy, it sounded quite comical to me though as Maggie had to stand on a chair in order to reach, what on earth was Terry doing whilst she got up there? I felt quite smugly that they deserved each other.

In the meantime I had made friends with a lady called Tess and we had some good times together and spent a lot of time back and forth to Brighton at weekends as her daughter lived there. As it was an old stomping ground for me I enjoyed a few trips down memory lane though I was always aware that I may bump in to Milly down there and wasn't sure how I would handle it. It turned out that Tess knew her anyway as they were in the same line of business! What a small world, even smaller on the gay scene especially back then.

I was to bump into her again only I was alone and it was in a club in London that I hadn't been to before. It was low lighting as most of the clubs were, I'd ordered my drink and then had a look round deciding if I was going to stay at the bar or find a table. There was a crowd at the far end of the bar and when someone moved there was Milly large as life with the usual entourage she used to attract surrounding her. I felt quite shaken it was the first time I'd seen her since we split up. Did I ignore her, or walk up as if nothing had ever happened and say hello, in the event I took too long to decide and the moment was gone I lost my nerve so decided to pay a visit to the loo and leave. I had to walk past them to get to the toilet and I probably was hoping she would make the move and talk to me, she didn't and I left. It upset me a lot, so for all I'd been up to one way or the other I wasn't as over her, as I thought and it hurt.

Revenge?

Well the evening came when the terrible two were to play a match against us in our own pub. I dithered about whether to go or not but decided I shouldn't hide and given some of the knowledge I'd gleaned from her daughters partner I must say I was curious to see how they were together.

When they arrived they sat as far away as possible from where we all were and just came up when it was their turn to play. I must say they didn't look very happy or particularly loved up, but that may have been the fact that I was there. A little devil started rising up in me and I didn't seem able to control it. I wasn't in the least bothered by them, which was a real plus, so I was being my usual self and having a laugh and a joke with everyone and totally ignoring them. I was up at the bar getting a drink and Maggie sidled up to me, a quick glance across the room confirmed that Terry was sitting there giving daggers in our direction. I thought "oh joy, what goes around comes around" and went all out in the charm and flirting stakes and was chuffed to find it was working. After a while I tentatively asked her would she like to have lunch with me the next day, she gushed that it would be wonderful, so it was arranged. All I really wanted to do was rub Terry's nose in it and show her how hurtful it was to be cheated on.

Oh dear, I don't know if I was born stupid or it just came naturally as I got older but after having a very civilised lunch we ended up arranging to meet again! That was the slippery slope right back into a full-blown relationship, dates at first for a while and then the moving back in with me.

Of course there were all the usual protestations of undying love and "I don't know what I was thinking of when I had who I really wanted all the time!" Of course being human (and stupid) I soaked it all up like a sponge, what an ego, what an idiot. I still thought a lot of what she was like was due to the terrible childhood she had and I tended to make excuses up for her in my mind as to why the grass always seemed to be greener for her on the other side. So off we went again another honeymoon period for a few months before settling in to a more humdrum existence.

Someone told us about a new club just for girls so we thought we would give it a whirl, it wasn't in our area so a bit of effort was made to go there. It seemed quite nice and the woman on the door seemed very pleasant and friendly, good start. We had found a nice table and were looking around to see if we knew anyone when the nice woman from the door came and asked if I would mind if she asked my lady to have a dance? I could hardly say no especially as I've already mentioned my dancing prowess was more or less non-existent. As usual it started off with a fast one and then switched to a slow one, which happened to be 'Lady in red', funnily enough Maggie was wearing a mainly red outfit that evening. I watched them and didn't like what I was seeing they looked very cosy for two people who didn't know each other; my warning bells were going off like mad. They didn't go near each other the rest of the evening and I thought I was just being unreasonably jealous but decided we wouldn't be making the effort to go to that particular club again.

A little time passed and I was still wandering around in my fool's paradise thinking everything was fine and dandy. I came home from work one evening to an empty house; it didn't feel like no one was in, it felt empty! When I went upstairs to get changed I found out why, all her clothes were gone and Daniel's, I couldn't credit it we had been fine not even arguing! I didn't find out till a few days later where she was, when her daughter rang to let me know. She'd gone off with the woman who danced with her at the club. I was amazed at when they'd even had chance to exchange phone numbers that night but it must have happened pretty quickly. So I did right to hear warning bells I should have believed my instincts. By this time I suppose I was getting used to it so I didn't go on the rampage this time I just shrugged my shoulders and got on with it.

Time passed by and one of Maggie's daughters told me the (new woman) had bought Daniel a school uniform for his new school, so I thought at least his welfare is being looked after and tried to get on with my life as best as I could.

I went to see the council to ask could I have an exchange for a one bedroom flat. Thinking If I didn't have room for more than one person beside myself it may stop me being stupid again, also paying double rent again was becoming a struggle that I could do without. They agreed that as soon as one came up I would have priority so it was just a case of waiting.

I began to think she was a witch, as soon as I felt like I was sorting myself out she'd pop back up again one way or another. This time manifested itself in a very distressed phone call at work from Greece! I wouldn't mind but it was Lesbos where she was staying so I could sort of see the funny side of it. I couldn't make a lot of sense of what she was saying and wasn't sure whether it was the shock of hearing from her like that or perhaps she was drunk (definitely a possibility), the gist of it was she was sorry and wanted to come back to me! I thought maybe she'd had a spat with her new girlfriend and would make up the next day, so I told her I couldn't talk when I was working and to ring when she got back to England.

She did, from the airport whatever had gone amiss must have been pretty serious, and she must have shown the new girlfriend a few of her true colours. Anyway I was a bit on the spot so told her she could come and see me but not to bring Daniel or her luggage as all we were going to have was a conversation. This was me trying to be grown up and sensible!

She arrived at the appointed time alone and full of contrition and pleading to come back. I said I wasn't prepared to have her back till she had proved she could stand on her own two feet without whichever available woman was there to prop her up. She always seemed to have the next person lined up when she left whomever she left and I wasn't prepared to do that again. I said she needed a place to live and a job before I'd even consider taking her back, so with that ultimatum burning in her ears she left.

She'd never worked since we met, but as Daniel was not so dependant I didn't see why she couldn't make the effort.

The next day at work I had a phone call from the council, it sounded like a fairly young man and he asked if I knew Maggie? I said I did and what came next had me flabbergasted he was asking me if I'd be willing to take her back. I thought this has to be some sort of joke and she'd got someone to ring pretending to be a housing officer so I took his name and phone number and said I'd ring him back off the switchboard. Well it was definitely the council and he was trying his best to convince me to forgive her and take her back, what a cheek! I asked him if he was married and he said yes so I said put yourself in my position and told him some of the history, then asked would you have her back. He agreed he wouldn't but in the meantime he had this weeping woman in his office and didn't know what to do about it. I said it wasn't my problem and wished him good luck.

If someone else had said that happened to them I wouldn't have believed them, she certainly knew how to manipulate people. The upshot was they put her in a bed and breakfast hotel in Victoria until somewhere became available. I said she still had to get a job and sort herself out all that had changed so far was the council were looking after her. She enrolled Daniel back in his old school near me which meant she had to make the journey from Victoria and back every day, which gave her ample time to hang around and see me when I came home from work. I did go and see the room they had put her in at the hotel and must say it was horrible, right at the top of an old Victorian building very tiny and roasting hot. You didn't actually get the breakfast they mentioned in the (bed and breakfast context), there was a tiny cupboard in the room with a kettle and they provided a loaf and butter every few days. It was dreadful but I still tried to stick to my guns but softened enough to let them stay with me at weekends, more for Daniels sake than anything else.

Eventually she got a job in an office in a small firm not far from where I lived, I was amazed that she'd followed through and had to stick to my side of the bargain and let her back, She was able to drop Daniel off at school on her way to work but wouldn't have been able to let him find his own way back if she'd still been in Victoria. A lady on my landing had two boys in the same school so she was able to look after him till one of us got home. So there we were back to being a family once again.

A Change Of Life

All during these events I was still enjoying my work at New Zealand House as well as the many social events that took place. I used to have to make sure all my Christmas shopping was done and dusted by the end of November as there was a party nearly every day from the sixth of December right up until Christmas eve, because we worked on the switchboard we were invited to every departments party and the whole month used to pass in a bit of an alcoholic haze. I once woke on the back seat of a bus that had finished its route and was in Croyden garage, luckily there was a cab firm across the road so I was able to get home. Another time I woke up on a bus and when I went downstairs there was only myself and the driver, it turned out I was in Lewisham and the bus was just changing over to a night bus, again I was fortunate as it passed through Vauxhall and I was able to walk the other three miles home. It was three in the morning when I got home and I was amazed to find Maggie still up. She went straight into attack mode and accused me of being with someone else, a thing I'd never done and she knew it. The real reason she was up was to explain where our puppy had gone that we'd got from Battersea dogs home a couple of months earlier. I'd said we could have one against my better judgement as Daniel had pleaded for one, as usual the novelty had worn off after a couple of weeks and I ended up being the one to do everything, Maggie was frightened of dogs and wouldn't even take it for a walk for fear of the pup attracting bigger dogs to it. Consequently there were some accidents indoors as we were on the seventh floor and it had a long time to wait when I was at work, so she'd got fed up and marched it back to the dogs home in a fit of pique, she knew I'd be furious so I'd played right into her hands being late that night.

My fortieth birthday was approaching and I decided nice as my job was I didn't want to work there another twenty years to my retirement, so a bit tongue in cheek I decided to apply for a job on the buses, thinking I'd spent so much time on them one way or another I may as well get paid for it! My application was successful and I started my new career as a clippie.

It was a bit daunting at first as you only had a couple of days training at Chelsea, where you was shown how to use a ticket machine and taught about different stages on the various routes which was very sketchy as nobody knew what route they'd be on at their garage. We were kitted out with our uniforms as well then sent off for a couple of days with another conductor from what would be your own garage. My garage was Victoria, which was Ideal as it wasn't far away from my home.

The only way you can really learn the job is just get on and do it, a bit frightening at first especially when people didn't know their way very well and would ask if you would tell them when to get off. I soon found out if I was nice to the regular passengers they would be only to willing to help me out with what stop was where. I'm sure I missed quite a lot of the stages at first so quite a few people were probably paying the wrong fare, they soon let me know if I charged too much but weren't so eager when it wasn't enough.

The routes I was to be on were the "11 and 19", One was more like a tourist route as it ran from Hammersmith all through Chelsea, which of course the Kings road and Sloane square were quite well known, then of course through Victoria and past the houses of parliament, the Strand and the Aldwych. All these places were of interest to visitors who wanted to be put off at specific places. I soon got over my initial shyness at shouting out the different places and ended up more like a tour guide as I got into the swing of the job. I loved every minute of it, though the first few months I thought I was going to die from exhaustion, the old hands assured me it would pass after the first six months and it did. One of the plus factors was I lost a lot of weight but didn't realise how much till I dropped another coin in my pocket on a very busy day and my trousers dropped round my ankles! The bus was in uproar I couldn't hide my modesty as whichever way I turned someone would get a bird's eye view of my backside, so I just bent over and hiked them up and a very kind lady gave me a safety pin. Of course if I'd have realised that you was supposed to bag your money up and put it in your little locker my pockets wouldn't have been so heavy and over flowing, just another bit of learning on the job.

You didn't get your 'own bus and driver' till you had been there a while and a lot of your time at first was spent waiting in the canteen on standby, a lot of cards were played and I used to do quite well as we played for money and I'd been weaned on cards when I was small. The down part was if you was allocated a bus after you'd been there about six hours you still had to go and do the full shift, so everyone was very relieved when they got their own driver and bus.

It didn't take long to get to get used things, knowing your route became second nature, so pretty soon everyone was being charged the correct fare. When I went to the training school they said we would have to watch out for (twirly's) whatever they were, I soon found out it was the pensioners with bus passes, they weren't allowed to use them in the rush hour and if it was about ten minutes before the cut off time they used to still flag the bus down and say "are we too early?"

Hence the t'w'early! If I had space on my bus I used to let them on as I didn't have the heart to leave them standing in the cold, It was quite funny as they got to know who was on what route and must have spread the word amongst their fellow pensioners as I seemed to have the bulk of them watching out for me. Another example, on the Kings road in Chelsea one of the bus stops was right outside a supermarket. The old saying about waiting ages for a bus and then three turning up at once was true, we used to somehow get bunched up because of traffic conditions and often turn up together until an inspector could come and reroute us so we would be back on time. Quite often two or three of us would stop outside the supermarket and I could see the old girls scanning each platform to see who was on and then I'd hear, this is the one with the nice lady on and they'd all come tottering towards my bus laden with their shopping bags, yes they could see a sucker from a mile off, I always used to lift their bags on and off and help them get seated properly before ringing the bell for the driver to go. It wasn't just me that was daft I often worked with Mick as my driver and if he saw a regular struggling along the road he'd stop and pick them up in between bus stops I even saw him get someone out of their wheelchair and carry them on to the bus and stowing the chair then the same in reverse when they got to their destination. Mind you he did that one night when I was going to a fancy dress party with him and his wife and son, he saw someone struggling to get out of their car with a wheelchair beside it, before you could blink he'd gone and lifted him out and deposited him in the chair only to find out the guy was in the process of getting into the car and his wife was going to put the wheelchair in the boot when she'd locked their front door! Fortunately they saw the funny side of it and we all had a good laugh, especially as Mick's fancy dress consisted of a black and white old fashioned swim suit that went down to his knees and over the shoulders with goggles on and a snorkel dangling round his neck, the bloke must have wondered what was advancing on him it was no wonder he didn't say too much.

I couldn't understand why there always seemed to be Saturday afternoon duties available and yet you could have the night time shift off with hardly any problem. I soon found out, again I was at the end of the Kings road in Chelsea we were at a standstill as the traffic was heavy, all of a sudden I heard a massive roar it was quite primeval and scared the wits out of me two little old ladies with small dogs under their arms scrambled on to my platform with as much haste as they could muster and managed to get behind me. I wasn't feeling particularly brave or protective but could hardly sling them off. Minutes later a hoard of young men wearing West Ham colours came hurtling round the corner quickly followed by Fulham supporters in full throat and chase! They passed by pretty rapidly and I must say for once I was quite relieved that we were stuck in a traffic jam; I had no desire to catch up with them. So there was the answer why none of the men wanted to do Saturdays, they didn't want to be in the cross- fire. The old ladies got off the bus thanking me profusely. Eventually we got moving and when we reached the next stop there was a big queue of both fans, with my heart in my mouth I ushered one lot upstairs and kept the other lot downstairs thinking I was going to have problems, I didn't. They were each singing their different anthems on each deck and though it became louder and more competitive by the minute it was all done in good spirit, most of them disembarked at Victoria and all gave me a peck on the cheek as they left. I'd learnt a valuable lesson, go with the flow and don't try and bully people into submission. I was quite lucky as a conductor it was at a time when other conductors were having problems some were even stabbed but I seemed to glide through my shifts with no problems, I think a lot of the time you get what you give, I was always even tempered and friendly and that's what I seemed to get back.

I used to have a lot of American tourists on and off on my route and as I became more confident used to give them the guided tour when I wasn't too busy. I often was given tips, which tickled me; I don't think they do that in the states. One night I was on my last run in to the garage so was obviously happy it was nearly home time, we picked up outside the Aldwych theatre and I was having a laugh and a joke with the few passengers that were on, as a couple were getting off the lady said in a very loud American voice "gee Harold give that girl a tip she was more entertaining than the show we've just seen", I was chuffed when he stuck a fiver in my hand.

When I was cashing up one day I was asked to go in the office when I'd finished, I went in full of trepidation wondering what I may have done, strange how we all feel guilty as soon as someone in authority asks to see you. It was far from trouble someone had written in singing my praises at how I'd looked after someone on my bus, saying how kind and considerate I'd been, not to the person writing the letter but he'd felt it shouldn't go by without mentioning it. I couldn't remember one incident in particular at all as I always tried to be helpful but management wanted my permission to put it in our magazine, fame at last.

Extra Stress

During this period things were going on fairly well with our relationship no big dramas everything seemed to be going reasonably smoothly. Along the way both Maggie's daughters where building their families, two boys for one and two girls for the other. This is when baby-sitting duty kicked in and normally it was only one or two at a time. One particular weekend they must have all been doing something at the same time and we ended up with all four at once. Everything was going fine until we reached the bedtime stage, that's when territorial rights seemed to kick in. Danny was about seven then there were three toddlers and a babe in arms. All hell broke loose in the bedroom, first of all it was just playing which we let them get away with for a while, and after all it was exciting having a sleep over all together for the first time. Then it started to sound like everyone was getting cross, I went up and found it hard to keep my face straight when Danny asked could he go in our room as he wasn't going to be able to get any sleep with all this going on! So he was transferred to the next room, not any quieter as we could hear it all over the house but he felt he had the high moral ground and noisy or not he eventually went to sleep, not so the holy terrors, I was up and down the stairs like a yo-yo. One would stop another would start; Maggie had already got well and truly stuck into the vodka so it looked like I was on my own! Being an only child doesn't prepare you for this. Having made sure they were safe and only being naughty I thought I'd just turn the music up and let them get on with it, before I did I left a cassette recorder playing just outside the door to show the girls what little devils they'd been. When I played it back the next morning it was hilarious, they seemed to have suddenly gone a bit quiet and then the three toddlers had started to plan their escape it was like listening to a juvenile episode of Colditz. I've heard of wicked stepmothers but we seemed to have taken on the role of wicked grandparents. They'd forgotten all about it in the morning and as kids will, they were all bright and perky waiting for their next adventure and we were half dead. Luckily we were only across the road from Battersea Park so a picnic was thrown together and we spent the day there and managed to wear them out so a peaceful night was had by all and we got some sleep. We never looked after them all together again!

Maggie had been for a smear test and was called back as there were some abnormal cells, it was all very frightening at the time and to make matters worse they said she would have to wait for a hysterectomy which of course meant lots more time to worry.

Daniel was on his way home from school and ran across the side road without looking and a car reversed into him, fortunately she was going really slowly and felt the bump so drove forward, his belt was tangled with the bumper so he was dragged forward with the car. He was in St Thomas' hospital, they didn't think he was too bad but kept him in for observation for the night. We'd no sooner got home than Maggie had a haemorrhage, an ambulance was called and she was taken to St George's hospital and kept in. Luckily I was on an early shift the next day so went straight to St Thomas to see Daniel expecting to be bringing him home. He seemed very distressed when I arrived and the nurse said he wanted to go to the toilet and was refusing to get out of the bed because it hurt. She obviously thought he was playing up for attention but I knew better than that, he could be a little sod but he wasn't soft. One of the doctors came in the ward so I asked if he could check Daniel over and explained his mum was in another hospital so it was down to me. When he put the x-ray up to check it turned out he had a crack in his pelvis and wasn't surprised that it was hurting. There was nothing to do but give it time, as he was so young. It was to cause him trouble all through his growing up years and last year aged thirty-five he had his hip replacement at long last. So off I went to see Maggie in the other hospital she was straining at the bit to come out but they wouldn't let her just yet. When I finished work the next day I went to see Daniel only to find he had gone home with his mum. When I got home she said she had discharged herself as she was worried about Daniel which is understandable but what was really stupid was she'd lifted him in to a bath and sure enough a couple of hours later she was on her way back to hospital bleeding again! The upshot was her operation was brought forward so in a cock-eyed sort of way it was a good result.

The company she was working for was only very small and they couldn't hold her job open for her for the three months she would be off, they were very nice people and very apologetic but it meant when she was better we would be back to square one. Anyway I nursed her through it and did all the heavy stuff so she made a good recovery. By this time I'd been on the buses nearly a year and when I started I'd put my name down to be a driver if possible and about then my name came up.

The first day of training dawned there was to be one more pupil and our instructor. When we gathered in the garage to start off I thought we would be driven to Chelsea where there was a skid pad for training, wrong again I was chucked in the driving seat, given a quick rundown on what was what and told to start the engine and drive out of the garage, "I haven't driven anything for four years" I squeaked! No notice was taken and I was told to get on with it. The good news was my destination was to some quieter stretch of road but I had to get there first. Although the buses were mainly automatic we had to learn to drive them in gears, I really couldn't get to grips with why you had to accelerate to change down, it just didn't seem logical to me and still doesn't. The only contact we had with our instructor was him talking to the back of our heads through the space where the window used to be. I'm sure the general public would have been very afraid if they'd known what was bearing down on them in the shape of a double decker route master with L-plates. Anyway somehow or another we were managing to get through it relatively unscathed, I did frighten a bloke to death in Brixton who had a big posh Mercedes double parked on yellow lines on the main road, I missed his wing mirrors by a fag paper, not sure what he was saying but am sure it wasn't very complimentary and I never knew anyone could turn that colour without passing out.

One day we'd stopped for lunch in Croyden garage, when we set off again he said I had to turn right out of the garage take the first left and then left again, each turning was very near and I was so busy looking for the turning I didn't see the sign saying it was a one in five gradient! When I turned I was confronted with a big steep hill, I did what most learners would have done, put my foot down and tried to race up it before it realised I was there! My instructor was screaming for me to put my foot on the break and slow down (never knew a man's voice could go so high), I was frightened to take my foot of the accelerator in case we rolled backwards, I felt like the bus was going to come unglued from the road and flip upside down, I was truly petrified at this stage and screaming at him as loud as he was screaming at me, the other pupil who was a half caste boy had turned completely white. Somehow I managed to get to the top, at this stage I was a gibbering wreck, crying, shaking and furious. I jumped down from the cab and told him in no uncertain terms what he could do with his bus and stormed off to find a bus route to get me home. The bus I got on and the driver seeing I was distressed tried to calm me down and asked what happened after I'd told him he said there was no way he should have told me to take that turning without a warning and a little instruction. I was only ten days into my driving course but I was determined to pack it in, I went in the next day to do just that. My instructor pleaded with me not to as he said the inspector would insist on taking me out and I'd go and do everything perfectly and he'd look stupid. I still wanted out I hadn't felt in control in any way the day before and my confidence had been knocked sideways. The inspector did take me out and I did all right he talked me out of packing it in so I carried on. Fate intervened, I had been waiting for years for a hysterectomy as I'd had problems since I was fifteen and out of the blue I had a letter saying there had been a cancellation and if I was willing I could have the operation in three days, it fell on the day I would have had my driving test, I didn't hesitate and opted for the operation. It was perhaps a blessing that I didn't become a driver who knows, I had to go to the bottom of the waiting list so it would have probably been another year before I had another chance.

The operation was a success and after six days I was back home, my mum was staying to help out, as I had to recover. Maggie had managed to get herself another job locally in a small office that just consisted of a father and son and was probably pleased to be out of the way so she didn't have to look after me. I recovered very well and my mum went home. My birthday was looming and a friend of ours who lived in Folkstone said her and her girlfriend would come over and treat us to a meal. They arrived in the afternoon and we booked a taxi to pick us up in the evening. Maggie was going to the hairdressers on her way home from work, so I had a bath already run for her when she came in, all she had to do was get ready. She was complaining of a pain in her jaw, but the previous week she had an abscess so I thought it might have been that lingering especially as she was rushing about. The taxi came and off we went, we were going to the West End and as we approached our destination we saw a lot of police activity and eventually we were flagged down and told there was a bomb scare and we would have to make our way to the restaurant on foot. At least it wasn't raining I have a May birthday and we used to have spring weather then. When we arrived it was a Bavarian restaurant and seemed very nice, Maggie still had her pain and I was hoping it would pass off and not spoil the whole night for us all. It seemed to and we enjoyed a lovely meal, Jan was a bit of a show off and insisted we had loads off photos taken by the professional that was there, why have one? When you can have half a dozen. The same with the drinks we had cocktails we'd never heard of, but I was pleased to see Maggie had cheered up and was even dancing, (the gay Gordon's of all things, not much to do with Bavaria). After that they did do their regional dancing which amongst others involved the clapping song, which was performed with much gusto, and we were all expected to join in. It had been a really enjoyable evening and was drawing to a close; we had coffee, liqueurs and the bill! That's when everything went downhill, Mrs Scattercash (Jan) didn't have enough money to pay it, not by a long shot. I hadn't brought any out with me as I was told not to as I was being treated, should have known it was too good to be true. I had to send her home with my keys to get my credit card, her friend went with her and we were left feeling more and more uncomfortable as time passed by. Maggie had started to feel ill again and thought she was going to be sick so had to go to the to the toilet, she was gone a long time but I daren't go to see how she was as we were in a basement and to get to the toilet you had to pass the stairs that led to the street, they may have thought we were going to do a runner. It seemed forever but eventually they turned up and I paid the bill. She gave me what money she had and I ended up about sixty pounds out of pocket and still had to pay the taxi home! Some birthday treat, she said she would pay me back but never did.

While we had been waiting for them to return another thing that Maggie was doing was drumming her feet, I thought it was just because she was getting anxious, I know I was. When we got home she went straight up to bed whilst I sorted them out on a bed settee and paid the baby sitter. When I got up there with a cup of tea for both of us she was still drumming her feet and looked awful, I thought she'd probably drift off and be alright but it didn't stop. I phoned for the emergency doctor, when he came he checked all her vital signs and everything seemed all right but because he didn't know her or her history he called an ambulance. They checked her as well and all the way to the hospital, she was ok no signs of anything. We'd been there about ten minutes and I saw them flying in and out of the cubicle, she had a heart attack fortunately not a large one. When they got her on to a ward and did some tests they could see she'd had one earlier and when I said she'd been sick they said that was probably when it happened. All this time she was fully conscious and chatting, I thought I'd better head for home, as

Daniel would wake up and wonder why we weren't there. I asked the ward sister what the prognosis was as I would have to tell her children, she said as I wasn't related she couldn't tell me. I told her I was her partner but she said it didn't count, I was furious being counted as a nonentity again just because I was gay. I went to say cheerio but as I was going a nurse came and brought me a cup of tea as I'd already been there for hours it was a bit of a surprise but it would have been churlish not to drink it. Then there seemed to be lots of activity going on around the machine and a specialist came down. I thought perhaps I was in the way so said I would go home and sort Daniel and come back with some things for her later on. As I walked down the corridor the unhelpful sister ran after me and said I had better prepare the kids as she was just in the middle of another heart attack and this was a major one! I went home in a daze and set about letting the girls know. It was definitely a birthday to remember but for all the wrong reasons!

She was in hospital nearly three weeks, I spent most of the time running to and fro visiting and looking after Daniel all at the time I was supposed to be recovering from my operation, I wasn't feeling super fit! On a holiday the previous year I'd won three six berth caravans at the same site and the same week at Beestons holiday camp in Devon. I had allocated one each to the two girls and we were to have the other one, I didn't think we'd be going given the situation but Maggie had told the doctor about it and was stressing so much about wasting the holiday that he said it would be more beneficial for her to go than worry about it so long as she was sensible and didn't do too much. I on the other hand was worried sick that she'd pop her clogs on the holiday so wasn't looking forward to it at all. Her youngest daughter had assumed that we wouldn't be going and let her husband spend their holiday money on a new engine for a car he was doing up so we wasted one anyway as it was too short notice to give it away. We took my friend Mick's son with us for a bit of company for Daniel, as we weren't really in a fit state to be entertaining. We went by coach and I arranged for her to sit at the front just in case there was an emergency (not the best way to start a holiday) I was on pins all the time till we got there. Her other daughter and partner had come by car which was just as well as when we arrived we discovered the caravans were right at the bottom of a steep hill, about as far away from the amenities as you could get. So he ferried   belongings and us down there. He was only stopping the night and coming back to pick them up at the end of the week so I had visions of us being trapped at the bottom of the hill for the week! As luck would have it we made friends with the people on the other side of us and one of them was recovering from an illness so they drove us up to the top for our evening meal, they had a game of bingo then went back to their van taking Maggie back to ours at the same time. I could manage to walk down the hill but not up it so was at least able to stay and have a few drinks, which I really felt I needed as my nerves were shot to bits. As holidays go that was the worst I've ever had I was so pleased to get home. When we went to see the specialist on our return he said the person who was looking after the patient in this situation was probably worse off. He wasn't wrong, I felt wretched and she looked healthier than she had for a long time. Mind you she did chose that time to tell her employer not to hold her job open as she wouldn't be coming back, though the specialist said she would be fine to go to work. She never worked again whilst she was with me as far as I know she never did again.

A couple of months went by and we were recovering well when I had a phone call from my mother's neighbour to say she had found her collapsed behind her front door and she thought I'd better come and see her. I went straight away and by the time I got there she had more or less recovered, she'd had a very bad bowel blockage and it had taken her nearly two days to get down the stairs, her phone wasn't working as she hadn't paid the bill she'd got as far as the front door and collapsed. It was pure luck that Iris found her; she needed to ask her something and knew my mum didn't go far without letting her know. After making sure she was ok and sorting her phone bill out I went back. I made sure I talked to her every day to set my mind at rest. I had a long think about it and decided I wasn't doing anything in London that I couldn't do in Manchester. The only regular thing we did was belong to a darts team, which you can do anywhere and my raving about days were well and truly over. Didn't even go to the theatre anymore, so why not move?

I went to see the council and arranged to go on an exchange list, didn't really hold out much hope but the alternative would have been to move in with my mum and given it had taken all those years to gain my freedom from her I didn't want to go down that road. I was amazed to hear about one pretty soon and even better it was in Swinton, which was only four miles away from my mums. Back we went to Manchester to view it; I was a bit shocked when I went in as it had a huge hole in the living room ceiling with laths hanging down. The living room was full of washing machines and cookers and the main bedroom had about twenty televisions in it all plugged in and in various stages of working! He was obviously using it as a business and as it was a mid-terrace in the middle of a council estate I didn't know how he was getting away with it. I could see the potential and assumed the work would have to be done to it before the exchange took place, so we went to the council offices together and made the preliminary applications, he wasn't happy when I went to the repairs department and told them what needed doing. I realised afterwards that it would have meant him getting rid of all his repair jobs before he could let anyone in.

Everything went through pretty smoothly but a lot of the business with the council was done over the phone, as at the time there was a postal strike. My property was given a real going over by the inspectors to make sure it was fit for exchange so I was very confident the same was happening in Manchester. The day of the exchange was the twenty ninth of September, which I thought was strange as that had been my discharge date from the army, I thought it must be fate? I wasn't going to move in yet as I didn't really want to pack my job in till I had another one lined up, easier said than done.

I hired our removal van from Manchester thinking their local knowledge on how to get there would be best. We did a deal and he picked up the belongings of the guy we'd exchanged with, must say it wasn't what you'd expect, six tea chests of tools nuts and bolts and goodness knows what, no clothes or furniture, very strange man.

When we set off they announced they had a package to deliver near where the stock exchange was and did I know the way? We were travelling with them in the van so that part wasn't a problem. We became totally lost trying to find our way to the motorway from there, there wasn't any sat-navs in those days just a well-worn atlas. If we'd have gone from home I would have been fine. Anyway it made a long day even longer as it turned out their local knowledge at the other end wasn't much better. We arrived at what was to be our new home at ten at night, when it was all unpacked we just threw ourselves onto the mattress all together (not the removal men) and conked out till morning.

Shambles

What a state when we got up! The living room ceiling still had a great big hole in it, with wires hanging down so no light in there. Everything had been painted in a very cheap brilliant white paint obviously to cover things up. I went to put the gas fire on, not only was there no gas but the fire had a condemned sign on it. Even though it was Saturday I managed to contact someone from the gas board and they were thrilled to hear from me as they had been trying to gain access to the property for nine years! What had this guy been up to and why didn't the council know about at least some of it? I couldn't do anything about the council till the Monday but was well revved up for when I did as I hadn't signed their agreement because of the postal strike so was only there on trust via telephone calls from them. The only good thing the guy had done was insert new plugs into every plughole in the house and lots of new light bulbs were lying around he must have had good supplies of both in his business. I had asked him if he would leave his phone connected so we wouldn't be isolated in case of another heart attack or any other emergency and when I made contact with the phone company they were aware and we picked up as new customers but with the same number. We moved in with my mum for the weekend and she looked after Daniel whilst we tried to sort out some of the unpacking.

Monday morning I was on the doorstep of the council when it opened. They looked like they didn't believe me when I said what a state it was in, they also said I would have to be responsible for a new fire as it wasn't one they'd put in, I said they'd better get in touch with the old tenant and tell him to come back then as I wasn't going to sign any agreement for a house that looked like it was all falling down. They agreed to replace the fire and fix the ceiling, so I said I wasn't signing till they had. So at least they got on with that bit and checked all the radiators when I said he obviously hadn't used them for nine years.

Unfortunately I had to get back to London as I couldn't have any more time off work as I'd only just got back after three months on the sick after my operation. I went and introduced myself to my next door but one neighbour who seemed very nice and she said she'd keep an eye out for Maggie and Daniel, as they didn't know the area. That gave me a little peace of mind and I went back to carry on with my job.

I was going to stay with Maggie's eldest daughter, the one with two little girls. It was quite a long way from Victoria so made my working days longer but I managed. We got on very well so the part of lodger wasn't a problem and I was able to help out with the girls when I wasn't at work.

Maggie and Daniel came to stop for Christmas and I can't quite remember what it was about but Maggie and her daughter had a big fall out, I was probably at work at the time, it must have been bad as my driver said we could stay with him till they went back. When they went back I continued to stay with him, as I would have felt disloyal going back to her daughters even though it was nothing to do with me, we still stayed friends though.

I was due to go back in hospital again for an operation on one of my toes, I thought it was only minor and I'd be in and out. I was in the hospital for ten days and wasn't allowed to put my foot on the floor for eight of them. I obviously wasn't going to go back to work anytime soon so one of the ladies at work arranged for me to go convalescent At the London

187

transport union hotel. It was a beautiful five star hotel and I had two weeks there I think it was in Eastbourne. They used to have conferences and seminars there so there was quite a good social life in the evening and as I couldn't hobble very far it was good.

I did have a little incident there which I found quite amusing, I'd been put in a twin bedroom and had to share with another lady who was getting over an operation, she was a bit of a moaner and a bit clingy, every-where I went she was two paces behind, everyone I spoke to she put her oar in and bored them to death. We were chatting in the room one night just before settling down and I must have mentioned my (girlfriend) not by design just came out naturally. She went very quiet for once and we settled down to sleep and I thought no more about it. When I woke up in the morning she was already dressed and on her way out of the room, strange, as she never made a move without me. I found out later she had gone to the management and kicked up a rumpus about having to share with a pervert and would they move me out? They didn't appreciate her attitude and moved her into a broom cupboard somewhere and left me where I was. She left a couple of days later, rang her daughter up to come and collect her. Everyone we had made friends with couldn't stand her because she was a whiner and only put up with her because of me, when they found out what she'd done they gave her the cold shoulder and made an extra fuss of me.

So back to reality and my driver's spare bedroom, I literally lived in there as the living room was in a state of half way to nowhere. It was bereft of any furniture and half stripped ready for decorating and had been in that condition for many months, he obviously didn't think it was a priority. He was a brilliant driver and put all the rest of his energy in to a wide range of lady friends, one of whom had just had his baby. He must have also been a very good juggler as somehow or other he managed to keep them all in ignorance of each other! Consequently I kept a very low profile when any of them were staying over for fear of putting my foot in it with a wrong name or something. My driver was a tall handsome black guy and all of his girlfriends wanted to know what he was doing with a (rhass clatt white woman in his flat?) Don't know if that's how you spell it but that's what it sounded like and I know it was derogatory. It was very nice of him to put me up but a strain trying to keep quiet and out of the way, especially as the walls were very thin and I could hear what went on with all of his conquests.

I went back to work as soon as I could and as time passed by it became apparent I wasn't going to be able to gain employment from long distance, maybe if I'd been a brain surgeon or the like but not an ordinary worker. So I bit the bullet and gave my notice in which was a sad occasion for me as I loved the job and got on with most of the people. The day I did my last duty fell on St Patrick's day and all the crew that were coming off shift at the same time as me insisted we go in the local pub near the garage, of course it was Irish so already bursting at the seams when we arrived early afternoon. I've no real recollection of leaving there just a slight memory of being carried out in someone's arms, but I woke up safe and sound in my drivers flat so I had been well looked after though not by my driver as he'd had to leave early, but he thought it was another lad I used to work with that brought me back. Anyway that was my farewell to London as well as the job and a couple of days later I was in my new home.

Skint Again

I soon found finding a job would be no easy feat, I registered at the employment straight away and was informed I couldn't claim any money as I gave my notice in, which I expected but mentioned in passing that I had moved because of my mother's health. To my great relief I was able to claim some money as I'd relocated to help mum. It wasn't a lot but better than nothing. We were already struggling as Maggie couldn't get any money in her own right for her share of the rent as they said as we were partners I was responsible for her, great! Couldn't be involved in decisions about health and not classed as a partner for that sort of thing but the government were quite happy to accept us being together if it saved them money!

Luckily as I'd been in the hospital Saturday fund I had received a cheque for the ten days I was in hospital and the two weeks in convalescence. This enabled me to buy a second hand car, to help me in my quest for work. It was a clapped out old banger but I thought it would get me from A to B. I nearly ruined it completely on my first outing, It was just when unleaded petrol came out and I didn't know the difference so filled it up with unleaded, didn't realise that because it was an old model it would have had to be adapted. Decided to take it for a run for me to get back into driving, as all I'd driven in well over four years was a double decker bus for two and a half weeks. So we set of for Southport as our destination as it was a lovely sunny April day. Got there with no problems and parked up on the promenade while we went for a stroll in the sunshine, there were a couple of children's rides open so Daniel had a few goes. On the way back to the car we treated ourselves to a cornet each, as we started off Daniel must have been clutching his too tight and the top half of the cone suddenly did a swan dive, well his face was a picture, he was so shocked and upset all at the same time, we couldn't help laughing and he got a strop on as he thought we were laughing at him unkindly, I tried to placate him and get him another cornet but he wouldn't have one and marched off in an indignant sulk. So I let him get on with it and he had to wait whilst we finished ours before setting off for home. Half way back on the approach to a roundabout the car refused to go any further, Panic set in as I hadn't had chance to join any rescue service, anyway after waiting a while it obliged us by starting and we limped home in that fashion, every time we had to stop at a junction or a traffic light the dam thing would play up, so not only did we have a stroppy awkward kid on our hands but the car joined in too. I found a nice garage the next day and he said there was no great harm done just to keep going till all the unleaded petrol had got out of the system.

After quite a few interviews for various jobs, I wasn't fussy just so long as a wage was involved I managed to get one in a petrol garage. It was a little tongue in cheek when they asked me had I any experience? I said a little a lot of years ago remembering the fiasco of putting wrong fuel in vehicles, thought it better not to go into it too deeply. It was a whole different ball game by then anyway as it had all gone self-service so the drivers of Manchester were going to be spared my assistance. The wage was dreadful minimum rate at that time was two pounds fifty pence and that's what I got; it was an eight-mile drive up the motorway so fuel to pay for as well! Still it was better than nothing and more than the dole. You had to do a stock take after your shift, everything in the shop and all the petrol readings, it was a pain but you soon got used to it. Unfortunately you were expected to do all the paperwork of the days takings after you closed at night time, I thought this was a bit above and beyond the call of duty for the measly wage we were getting but you just did what you was told and hoped for the best. I hadn't had to do anything as complicated even when I was managing the bakery in London. The garage closed at nine in the evening but I very rarely got home before midnight as I struggled to balance the books and I wouldn't leave till I got it right. I wrote a little poem about it;

I'm working on the petrol pumps
And it has got me in the dumps!
Sell the petrol, count the stock,
I've rung it wrong, oh what a shock.
Sell the ice cream, check the oil,
Not even time for the kettle to boil.
Sweep the floor and mop it up
Don't forget to wash your cup.
The time has come to count the cash,
I bet I'll make another hash.
I've done it once, I've done it twice,
This really isn't very nice!
It's turned out wrong, how can that be?
A repeat performance for twenty P.
I'll go home now, just for a rest
And tell my partner to get it off my chest.

That was a bit of fun but in reality I was getting more distressed about it by the minute and had to keep ringing home for help. Fortunately one of the jobs Maggie had in her distant past, long before we met was as bookkeeper in a car sales garage so she was able to help me. She did keep saying I shouldn't be expected to do book keeping on the wage I was on, but at the time I was just glad of a job.

My wreck of a car was still playing me up every time I stopped at a crossing or roundabout, fortunately I didn't have cause to stop on the motorway else I would have been in big trouble. It had electric windows, didn't take long to discover if the driver's side was opened it wouldn't close again, I often drove to work with my head sticking out of a bin bag in the pouring rain because some idiot (usually me) had inadvertently opened it. It also had a loose locking system, whilst at work I thought I'd check my tyres before going home, I got out, the door slammed shut, the lock went down and the engine was still on. This was on the forecourt of a petrol station, great! Next door to us was a car hire place and luckily for me they had a gadget for getting into a locked car so were able to rescue me on that occasion. I was so fed up with the window situation, I'd tried garages and they couldn't find out why it wasn't working, I got one of the lads from the garage on the other side of us to take the door panel out and prop the window shut with a broom handle broken in half, It could never be opened by accident again.

As time went by I was to discover why I had to do all this book keeping, someone commented on how long I had managed to stay in the job which I thought was strange as I hadn't really been there that long. They said people were lucky if they got past three weeks. It turned out the manageress was on the fiddle and the way she covered her tracks was blaming the last person to come to work there. Unfortunately for her I was stubborn and made sure I was doing the job properly, she also used to get rid of them by saying they were pilfering the stock which was easy to do when the book keeping was wrong. Behind the counter at the end was a little store room where the cigarettes where kept for stocking up, it was usually locked and my stocks were a bit on the low side so I asked for the key to stock up, she said to leave it for the time being. I found out why later, there was a man in there watching to see if I stole anything. So much stuff had gone missing and she tried the usual trick of pointing the finger at the latest recruit. To cut a long story short she had been on the fiddle for ages and this time they caught her out.

When the new managers took over, a husband and wife team, I think they had bought the lease. I just carried on and did what I'd been doing all the time, I was on the late shift so did the books as usual. When I went in the next afternoon they called me in to the office and asked me how long I had been doing the books? I said since I started, they were amazed and said it wasn't part of my job especially on the rate of pay I was on; it was a manager's job! They would be happy for me to cover them if they went on holiday, for managers pay but I didn't have to worry about doing it anymore, turns out I'd learnt how to do double entry book keeping without even realising it.

I did cover for them when they went on a holiday and satisfying as that was I really needed to find a job with better pay, as I was really struggling. What had actually been a manageable credit card bill took on horrendous proportions when my wages plummeted and the minimum payment was the equivalent of a week's wage in Manchester. Consequently I was robbing Peter to pay Paul and having to use the card for grocery shopping and day to day living.

I saw a job advertised at the airport garage and managed to get an interview, the wage was much better but it included night shifts, I didn't think I'd mind that as my past life included being up most nights, I think I may have been a bat in a former life. Bit further away for my old banger to negotiate, sixteen miles each way but she held out, my heart used to be in my mouth every time I set out in case we didn't make it.

Because the rate of pay was improved I trotted off to the bank and pleaded for a bank loan, I was a bit loathe to do it but the interest would work out much cheaper than the credit card interest. Thankfully they gave me one and that helped my situation enormously.

Our relationship was plodding along without too many problems, mainly as we weren't able to afford to go out anywhere we weren't meeting any new people so no temptations to stray anywhere on Maggie's part. Daniel seemed to have settled in his new school though at first he used to come home upset because they were calling him "the cockney ginger nut", he could sort of understand the cockney bit but not the ginger nut as he had blonde hair, but on the back of his head he had a very ginger patch of hair about the size of a biscuit and try as I might I couldn't manage to get him to see the back of his head in a mirror. One day we were walking along the road and I saw a man just about to get on the bus and he had jet black hair with a circle of pure white on the back just like Daniel's. I ran up and asked him to stop and when he saw what I wanted he didn't mind missing his bus in the least and he was really lovely with Daniel, he got down on his knees and showed him his white patch and explained that he had a lovely orange patch and it made them both very, very special. I could have kissed him, he said he'd had problems as a child so could understand it and didn't mind in the least. Peace reigned again at school and Daniel could stand up for himself and say he was special. He also tried very hard to pick up a Lancashire accent, which was quite comical at times.

My new job although better paid had its own set of problems, mainly on the night shift. Quite a lot of drive offs occurred, people nipping in from the nearest local estate to fill up and drive away without paying, it was pretty easy to escape as we filtered directly through to the motorway so there was a lot of that. The main thing that bothered me was you had to actually go out of the shop to use the toilet, this presented the problem of having to lock the shop up whilst you went but once outside you were totally exposed to someone grabbing hold of you and forcing you to open up so they could rob you. Not ideal, when I questioned it I was told the men had a pee in the sink and I could always use a bucket! A bit dark ages I thought, I also found out that they had been robbed in this manner quite recently, so I set about looking for new employment pretty quickly. My settling down in Manchester wasn't going very well, I felt a bit like when I first moved to London and was moving from one job to another, unfortunately there wasn't as many jobs available in the eighties as there had been in the sixties.

Eventually I saw a security guards job in the local newspaper so had an interview and off I went again. The wage again wasn't very good but the hours were longer which meant I could earn enough to pay my bills. I was based at a bedding warehouse and two of us worked together on the night shift and one on days with a sort of floating supervisor in the daytime. I had been asked was I willing to work over time when I started and of course said yes but when I was given my site it was five twelve hour nights which I assumed was enough to cover any overtime required, so when asked to do more I was politely saying no. Until someone said to me if you don't agree to do some extra shifts you'll lose your job! So I ended up doing six shifts and found that I was struggling to change from nights to days so ended up doing permanent nights, after a while I found it easier not to have a night off at all as I couldn't adjust to having just one night off and trying to sleep like a normal person. So for quite a while all I did was sleep, eat and work.

In the midst of all this job changing we had gone to London to spend Christmas at Maggie's youngest daughters. Before we even attempted the journey I had my car thoroughly checked out, even had new tyres, in fact spent a lot of money on it but as the MOT would be due in January when we came back I thought it was money well spent, HUH. On the end part of the journey on the way back copious amounts of smoke started gushing from the bonnet and when I pulled over to the slip road I was told by the man that came out to us from the rescue service it was minutes from blowing up! Great, I had a car full of our bedding that we'd had to take with us as well as all our presents and he wanted to tow us to a local garage and us get a train home for the last fifty miles. I had no money so would have been stranded, so had to plead with him to tow us nearer home. He was concerned that I wasn't used to being towed, I had to laugh I'd spent more time being towed in that car than actually driving it! He took pity on us and towed us to about two miles from home, I rang a taxi and when he saw the fix we were in he towed us home, I'd been hoping to leave the flipping thing behind and hope that someone stole it but no such luck. It had to go to the scrap heap and I was given twenty-five pounds for it, I'd paid over three hundred for repairs before setting off. I actually shed a tear when it was being taken away for all it had been a trial from start to finish it was the first car I had ever owned.

My Uncle Harry had lost his wife, she drowned in Blackpool and it was all very sad for him. He suddenly found he had all the insurance money and was frittering most of it away in the pub in his despair and a lot of his so-called friends were helping him go through it at an amazing rate. (He did calm down eventually and moved in with my nana). He came good for me and gave me a thousand pounds so I could get another car. That's when I became the proud owner of my lovely old Volvo. As I only had a license for automatic I was restricted on the type of car I could get and they were usually big ex company cars with thousands of miles on the clock, this was no exception but it was love at first site and even my favourite colour of pale blue. The Manager of the warehouse where I worked found it for me via his brother who was a dealer so I felt fairly safe that if it went wrong I'd have someone on the spot to moan at. Didn't expect the moment to arrive as soon as it did, the very next day I was driving in to work and I opened the window as it was a lovely day, when I got to work the window wouldn't shut! Oh no not again I thought, I marched straight into the factory and dragged the manager out he placated me and said he'd have a look on his tea break. It just needed a new fuse! I didn't even know cars needed fuses, you don't get a manual when you buy a clapped out old banger like my first and only car! The horrible thought dawned on me, had I gone through all that trouble with the other window and all it needed was a fuse? The mechanics would have probably expected me to have checked that for myself, of course I'll never know but if I'm concerned about anything now the first thing I do is check my fuses, you live and learn.

There were two of us on the night shift; I use the term loosely as I don't think my partner was altogether there at the best of times. One had to stay in our little cabin whilst the other checked the perimeter fences, you had to swipe a card through strategically placed clocks so you couldn't cheat and pretend to have done your patrol. The site was quite out in the open and we often found the fences cut through with wire cutters. It was a bit daunting, as you didn't know if the perpetrators were still on site and you were maybe going to get a crack on the head. That's why there was always one in the cabin watching the monitor as you did your rounds; it was supposed to protect you and give you comfort! I was living in a fool's paradise, we used to have a lot of police helicopter activity in the area and quite often I came back from my rounds to find my opposite number playing silly buggers and standing outside flashing the torch at the helicopter! When he wasn't doing that he spent the rest of his time on saucy phone calls, he was discovered when the company got a bill for nearly three thousand pounds! It was easy to check it was him as it was logged when we went on patrol and the calls always occurred when I was out. He didn't last long I'm pleased to say but it meant I had a succession of different partners night after night as they couldn't get a regular guard. I was still keeping an eye out for a better job all this time as it can get a bit wearing never having a night off.

A Proper Job

Eventually I saw an ad in the evening paper wanting a security guard in an Old Trafford food factory, I applied not holding out much hope as I thought the factory was Kellogg's and it was common knowledge that they paid good wages so thought there would be a stampede. It was a Soya mill, British Arkady which I found out when I got my letter for the interview.

When I went it turned out to be quite amusing, the chap who was in charge of the security squad was a Greek guy and it was obvious to me he had never conducted an interview in his life (I found this to be true later on), I sort of ended up interviewing him! The security part seemed pretty straight- forward but I was a bit concerned when he mentioned a weigh- bridge, I didn't even know what it was but assured him I was a quick learner and it wouldn't be a problem. I was given the job, there was a message on my answer phone before I even got home, so he was either impressed or desperate, I preferred to think it was the former. It was with great joy I gave my notice in to the slave drivers I'd been working for.

It was a mixture of day and night shifts but with enough time between to adjust to the change, a forty-eight hour week that paid me the same as I'd been getting for an eighty-four hour week. I felt more like I was on holiday than working. The day shift was mainly manning the weighbridge, which turned out quite easy so long as you were good at maths and it made the job more interesting. Nights you were completely on your own unless the factory had a rush on and needed a night crew to work. It was a big old rambling site that was part old- fashioned Soya mills and a modern factory and packing part. The main part of the business was making frozen dough for many various types of bread, which were sold in their deep frozen state to most of the big supermarkets up and down the country. So that lovely baked on the premises bread you smell in the supermarkets has probably originated from a mill in Old Trafford. I must say I was surprised as I thought it was all done from scratch at the stores. That was one of the main perks of the job as we had a test bakery and loads of samples of all the different types of bread were baked to test for quality. We were allowed to take as much as we wanted home they tried to give it to various charities but for whatever reason they wouldn't have it. All good for me and quite often I could take enough home to share with the pensioners on my mums estate. All of a sudden they were eating some very exotic bread that most of us hadn't heard of at the time. Occasionally they did an exhibition where people came from all over to test their wares, on these occasions there were lots of lovely cream cakes up for grabs and if you was the lucky one that was on the night shift you could take the lot, I was becoming very popular with the pensioners on my mum's estate.

In the meantime I actually had some free time, which meant we were able to have a night out now and again. Our neighbour who I'd introduced myself and Maggie to when we first moved in offered to take us to a couple of local pubs where he used to play darts and introduce us to the team captains. Seems silly that we'd been there that long and not been out but first of all it was money and then working every single night doesn't help. Anyway we managed to get fixed up with a dart team for the time being, we eventually changed as the ladies at the time played a really weird game and we'd been playing the way the professionals played for years so didn't really get on with the watered down version.

Still it got us out and we were able to make some new friends.

When we first moved there I'd kept the phone on in case of an emergency, I forgot to mention we had to change it as we kept getting phone calls in the middle of the night asking if we were "The Washing Machine?" It was usually businesses like Chinese restaurants and the like. We were very puzzled about this as mister Miller had been in London for quite a while and though we knew he had been using the house as a business we were a bit surprised to be getting late night calls. After a bit of investigating we found out we were in the local telephone directory as The Washing Machine! We couldn't get it removed so had to change the phone number. We also had quite a few visits from ladies looking for him and didn't get the impression they wanted anything fixing, one of them thought we were lying and we had to let her in to convince her we hadn't got him stashed away in the wardrobe! No wonder he wanted to move as far away as London.

Leo, our neighbour had a heart attack and because of Maggie we were able to offer a bit of help and advice. As a result we started to go to the local "Heart Foundation" club. It wasn't all doom and gloom, apart from practical advice we did a lot of different activities within the club and had a few outings. One of them was to Haydock horse racing stadium, it tickled me, as you'd think anyone getting excited about their horse winning could be a prime candidate for another heart attack. I'd never been to a horse race before and thoroughly enjoyed it. Daniel did too one of the ladies was letting him choose her horses for her and he picked nearly all winners, when she gave him half of her winnings he was over the moon. I just hoped the memory of early winnings didn't turn him into a gambler in later life. We also hired the use of a swimming pool for an evening weekly as the exercise is gentle and good for stimulating the heart. One of the older ladies had never been able to swim and was petrified of getting in the water at all. I had a long talk to her well before we went and she said she would trust me to take her in. I did and the very first day she swam three or four strokes. We were all highly delighted no one more so than herself. Her confidence rose and she never looked back or missed a week at the swimming pool.

Eventually we stopped attending as other things took over but Leo continued to go. We found through playing darts there were a few "sing along" pubs in the area, not karaoke just to an organ or piano the old fashioned way. I loved all that so now and again we went to them and took my mum. I made friends with a lady and her daughter who used to go to them as her chap used to sing and they did the circuit. It turned out she only lived down the road from me and we are still friends to this day.

Of course we eventually ventured into Manchester to the gay pubs and clubs but it didn't take long for the rot to set in. It seemed to me someone only had to give Maggie a complement or a sideways look and she was smitten, I don't think anyone ever taught her about loyalty or that the grass isn't really greener on the other side! Nothing as dramatic as her other performances in London happened but there was always something underlying. The feeling that you know dam well something's going on but you can't just put your finger on it, or more to the point prove it so there would be no point having a confrontation without any back up, how can you put a thing right if you can't prove its existence? She'd say she was going shopping in town (I hate shopping), set off in the morning and not come back till teatime. When she did she used to reek of drink, didn't have any shopping and say she just happened to bump into a friend and they went to the theatre. I never got a straight answer as to which friend it was; I mean we had met most of the people we knew together so if it was so innocent why not let me know. I wouldn't have actually minded if it had been so innocent. Part of me didn't want to rock the boat so I suppose I buried my head in the sand a bit. I think I was growing up a bit and couldn't be doing with all those confrontational moments, though there were a few more to come.

Maggie's youngest daughter came to stay for a few days and brought a Labrador pup with her from the litter her bitch had just had. I had said no way to another dog after what happened with the last one, of course confronted with it in my own home how could I send it back and it was as lovely little thing. Of course all the usual stuff, everyone initially was going to walk it feed it, that lasted a couple of weeks. I was the one that was getting more attached to it by the minute, I should have known better, it growled at Maggie one day in the garden and that was that she insisted we took it to Leigh dogs home. I was upset and furious but what was the point of keeping it when I was at work most of the time. I understood she was frightened of dogs, what I didn't get was her keep saying she'd have one knowing full well what the outcome would be.

At a later date her eldest daughter turned up to stay with us for a while as her and her partner had split up. Though it was delightful having the girls with us I was relieved when they got somewhere to stay, it was only a two-bedroom place one of which was very small, so fitting three adults and three children in was a problem, especially as Daniel was old enough to object to "girls" invading his space. She managed to get placed in a home for battered wives, I don't think she was for one

204

minute but it was a stepping stone to getting a council house especially as she had only just arrived in Manchester.

Wake Up Call

Time passed by and we had a few good times along the way, we went on holiday to Corfu and took my mum. That was where I had my moment as a paraglider; it was hysterical in the end. We went and put our names down for it as our hotel was right on the beach so we were on the spot and had seen that some people had gone up in tandem and thought we may be brave enough to do that. When they didn't come to get us after a while I went and checked and they said the wind was in the wrong direction for doubles! I accepted that and arranged for it for the next day. In the meantime a lot of the guests cancelled their trips the next day so they could watch us as they thought we were very brave (no backing out then).

The next day dawned to, much anticipation and excitement and still they never came for us, I went to see them and asked if it was because they thought I was too heavy to double up and I'd guessed right. So we went up solo! We had to swim out to a raft and be taken from there. Maggie went first, and went soaring up into the sky, then they did something that brought her back down so her feet were running across the top of the ocean then back up to the heavens again, it looked fabulous. Eventually they brought her back down and she had loved it. My turn next then, after much faffing about with a life jacket and the harness I was ready to go, they said when I was coming in to land they would give me signals what to do with my arms on the ropes and I would answer mirror image. Of I went and it was amazing, I could see for miles as well as all the people from our hotel waving like mad, the feeling of freedom was wonderful, then they tried to do the swooping down so my feet went in the water, they couldn't get me down far enough so I was a bit disappointed that hadn't happened but no time to worry about it they were bringing me in to land! They gave me the signal and I responded, nothing happened we did another circuit and they gave me the signal to do the same thing with more force, I did but still didn't come right down and they had to leap in the air and drag me down by the ankles, I landed on the raft in a big heap like a sack of spuds, I was in hysterics with laughter and they were trying to get me to stand up, I had neglected to tell them about my arthritis in my knees, I could only get up if I had something to push myself up with. There were four lads all grovelling about between my legs and round my boobs trying to get the safety harness off, as it was quite likely I would be dragged away at any minute, I was no use to them as I was helpless with laughter as was Maggie on the other side of the raft. They had miscalculated my weight, they thought I was a lot heavier than I was and that's why the ropes weren't acting like they should, that's why I shot off in the air when I pulled on it. We also found out afterwards that we should have told them Maggie had a bad heart and I had arthritis! Still I really enjoyed it.

My mum had one of her sleep walking episodes whilst we were there, I must have forgotten to lock the door and they found her wandering around the lounge looking for food, I was really pleased she didn't sleep in the nude that would have been a shock for the night porter, he just held her hand and brought her back to bed with a packet of biscuits.

Back to the reality of work and day-to-day living I was happy in my job, I mainly worked by myself, which I've always been quite content with. Even on the day shift you were left to your own devices to some extent. My security boss the one I interviewed to get the job was a bit of a dipstick who liked to think he knew it all but didn't, wasn't much of a force to be reckoned with so you may as well have been working alone anyway. It turned out the dreaded weighbridge that he asked me about at interview was a complete mystery to him most of the time and if you had to leave the lodge for a visit to the toilet you would be likely to come back to a queue of wagons waiting to be weighed in or out as he'd made a mess of it. He was all right with the incoming ones as you didn't have to do any calculations but when they were leaving he was stymied!

We started going out more to the gay village and I couldn't help noticing Maggie seemed much more interested with anyone or everyone so long as it wasn't me. This caused many an argument or full out screaming session at each other when we got home, then everything would be all right for a while then off we'd go again. I was just sat there one night watching the television and I thought this is no way to live for either of us. She would obviously be happy to be free to flirt to her hearts content and I had come to the conclusion that I didn't really care very much anyway and could do without all the confrontation. So much to her amazement I told her I was leaving and I would get the house signed over to her as she had Daniel and I could make my own way. I would initially stay with my mum whilst I decided what to do next. To say she was gob-smacked would be an understatement, I'd put up and forgiven her for all her past misdeeds and there I was finishing it when we weren't even arguing! I was a bit surprised myself, but resolute and off I went the very next day.

I went to see the council and told them a cock and bull story about having to move in with mum to look after her and would it be allowable for Maggie to carry on the rental of the house, they didn't see why not but of course it would eventually be formalised.

So I'd burnt my boats and for the first time in ages felt amazingly free of stress. It wasn't going to be that easy though. I had phone calls at mums and at work pleading with me to come back. She knew all my shifts so when on nights I couldn't dodge the calls, as I had to answer. Some of them were sober calls others she was drunk and maudlin, hanging up didn't seem to be an option as she would just ring back minutes later. That went on for a considerable time, when the phone didn't work she wrote me heart wrenching letters, she could be so convincing (which had always got me in the past) that I think she believed herself.

Eventually I had a letter telling me, as she obviously wasn't going to get me back she was moving out and I may as well get my home back! I wasn't sure if it was a ploy to get me there but when I gave in and went over she had gone. The next time she rang I asked her where they were as I obviously worried about Daniel and she informed me she was in Bolton in a home for battered wives! I said I dearly hoped she hadn't said I'd done anything like that but thankfully she hadn't. She must have told a string of lies to get in there though.

I went and grovelled at the council a little bit and told them my mum had made a miraculous recovery so I was going back home. It was all a little tongue in cheek as some of the ladies on the council were in my darts league and they probably knew more about what was going on in my life than I did!

Single Again

I didn't do anything different for a while just spent a period of adjustment getting used to being back on my own and I must say enjoying the freedom and sense of peace.

Whenever we had done any decorating I had been the one to do the helping as I wasn't considered capable of paper hanging! When I think about it now I have to laugh I did everything except the wallpaper and gloss, preparing the surface, painting the ceilings, measuring and pasting the paper and handing it up as well as cleaning the paper that I stripped off up. In between I would make all the drinks and cook all the meals. Afterwards she would tell everyone she had done the decorating. I thought I would give it a go but didn't feel over confident after years of that so asked my friend Margaret to give me a hand, as she was good at papering. I needed to do Daniels bedroom as it had "Red Devil" wallpaper on. Anyway when she came to help me she had me hang some of the paper myself and said it was fine, so I got my confidence back and found I was quite capable of doing it. Bit by bit I went through the whole house doing it the way I wanted it and I also turned into a bit of a "Percy Thrower" in the garden, much to my own amazement. I had a lot of help over a period of time from some of the ladies at work who brought me cuttings from their gardens so it didn't even cost me money just a lot of hard work. I was very content with my own company.

I still played darts and went to the sing along pub which I enjoyed so didn't feel lonely as I had many friends locally and didn't feel any inclination at all to go to the gay village, I'd had enough off girlfriends for the time being.

The young couple that used to live next door to me had left and the house had been empty for quite a while. I came home one day to see new neighbours moving in, the lady was in the front garden so I introduced myself to her and her husband when he came out. They seemed very nice but she kept looking at me in a strange way, I thought perhaps she was a bit anti-gay as I suppose I'm quite obvious, anyway I took no notice and we seemed to rub along ok. Many conversations carried on over the back fence when we were all working in our gardens. I did observe that if she didn't give him a break she was likely to kill him off and offered to take them with me to my local where the singing took place the next time I went, thinking it would help them to get used to their new area. Anyway they were very pleased to come and enjoyed the singing as much as I did and it became a regular event.

We were chatting one day when he was at work and it turned out she did think she recognised me from the past, when she worked at a gay pub in Eccles. It must have been once seen never forgotten as I only ever went in there once to meet a friend who lived round the corner. As the conversation progressed I was to find out she had a relationship with a woman for a few years at that time, after the break-up of her first marriage. As far as I was concerned she'd got over her gay fling, as she was married again. Occasionally when her husband was working away she would come to the pub with me on her own. He also came with me on his own when she went to some club or other she was in so it was all very easy going and friendly.

Bet you've guessed where this is leading! One night I'd had quite a good drink and realised she was flirting with me, they were both there but it was being done sneakily. I got a bit cocky and said she could always bring me tea in bed in the morning if she wanted, thinking she would sober up and have second thoughts! They had my door key in case of emergencies!

The next morning I woke up to the sound of his car door slamming as he went off to work, the memory of what I'd said came flooding back, I was desperate for a drink but didn't want to go and make one in case she did come in so I went and had a drink of water from the bathroom got back in bed and actually went back to sleep.

I woke up to see her standing over me "done up to the nines" with a big daft grin on her face saying "here's your naughty neighbour". Well it would have been rude not to really so away we went and I must say she'd made things really easy, a dress that had buttons from top to bottom at the front, when undone revealed some very saucy fishnet stockings and suspenders, it was shaping up to be a very exciting morning. I'm afraid I spoilt it a bit by saying I'd have to drink the cup of tea she brought me first as I was gasping. So that was the start of a very different interlude in my life. Being free and single wasn't all-bad.

I'd come home from work to find her in my house waiting to greet me, which was quite a novelty at first but it started wearing a bit thin when she was still in mine when he came home from work and was getting quite brazen about it. I thought she was out of line not even having a meal ready for him when he'd been at work all day and told her so. She was surprised at my attitude but it wasn't as if I was madly in love with her I was just having a dabble with someone who was handing it to me on a plate and didn't see why her husband had to suffer, I also didn't fancy the idea of him finding out. Often when we came back from the pub she would ask to come in and have a cup of tea before going to her own house and send him off to bed as he had to get up in the morning! I was amazed she got away with it but she did. My fiftieth birthday was nearly here and his birthday was only a week apart from mine, so she set about arranging a joint party for us at my house. It was a good night with loads of my friends and a lot of our neighbours. There didn't seem to be anyone special from their side but they were friendly with a lot of my friends from the pub so I don't suppose it seemed strange to him. He spent most of his time recording it on his birthday camcorder I still have a copy somewhere but I must say when I looked at it the main feature seemed to be me and his wife dancing together, I began to think maybe he was a bit kinky and liked the idea of us having a relationship. It was getting late and the party wasn't showing any signs of winding up so he excused himself and went home as he had to get up for work very early the next day. Once again she didn't in fact she didn't go home at all till after he'd gone to work the next day. I was sure there would be a row when he got home but she just told him she was drunk and fell asleep on a chair.

The affair carried on for quite a while, I wasn't bothered I was having all the fun and none of the responsibility. I'd made friends with a guy that used to sing at the pub, he was a character in his own right. He had an amazing voice that covered all ranges, one minute he would be belting out a country and western song then switch into a falsetto followed swiftly by something operatic. He looked more like a banker than a singer, always dressed in a silver grey three piece suit, bald head and side burns and the most expressive eye's I've ever seen in a man, he could have a conversation with you without speaking. In his younger days he had done warm up sessions in Las Vegas and had been on the same bill as Elvis Presley a few times. He said when he was doing his act he could see Elvis in the wings playing cards with some of his entourage.

He'd had an interesting life and was a lot of fun to be with. I'd met him not long before my birthday party and he was there on the night, he caught on straight away what was going on with my neighbour and was intrigued by it all. I used to go to Chorley where he lived and spend the weekend doing the rounds of different pubs and clubs he sang in, we had some fun times.

One night I'd come back from the pub with my neighbour a little worse for wear, he hadn't been out with us that night and of course she automatically came in with me for her bedtime cup of tea! This particular night we ended up getting passionate on the settee. I had sunshine windows in my house and we were in front of the one that faced on to the back garden, didn't have the curtains shut as there was no way anyone could pass as they were closed in gardens. I nearly had a heart attack when there was a hammering on the window and her husband shouting for her to get out of there! I couldn't believe how calm she seemed, she just stood up straightened her clothes, kissed me goodnight and said she'd see me the next day!

I thought discretion was the better part of valour and took myself off to bed and before long fell into a deep drink induced sleep. When I got up the next morning feeling decidedly worse for wear I discovered I needed a bottle of milk and as I staggered back from the shop with it she was hanging out of her living room window looking positively chirpy. When she came in for a cup of tea I was amazed to find out what had gone on when I was asleep. They had an unholy row that everyone in the street had heard except me, he'd started throwing all of her clothes through the bedroom window and she'd phoned the police and asked for protection, I wouldn't mind but she was about two foot bigger than him, the police sent a male and a female as it was a domestic, she implied that he had threatened her with a cup and when they asked what it was all about she said very bluntly "he caught me fucking with the woman next door". I don't think they really had an answer for that. When they left it was on the understanding there would be no more fighting that night. When he went to work the next day she told him only to come back for his clothes, as she didn't want him anymore! On top of that she'd already been out first thing and seen a solicitor about a divorce, talk about a fast mover. I had to put her straight pretty quickly and told her not to do any of this on my account as I didn't mind us fooling around but there was no way I was going to make a commitment to her.

I decided it was a good moment to make myself scarce for a while and went to my mate in Chorley for a few days. Turned out to be a good move as by the time I came back they'd made it up and all was rosy in their garden again. It was quite a strange situation from then on, he was happy to be friends with me but didn't want any of the neighbours to know so used to climb over the back fence to come in for a cup of tea and a chat. I thought it was a strange thing to do but assumed it was my glowing personality he liked plus he didn't have many friends. He even fixed my washing machine when it broke down. His wife on the other hand was full of animosity towards me, can't say I blamed her. They had three dogs and one of them used to howl when the phone rang, if it wasn't answered the other two used to join in. Quite a party trick, unfortunately for me it was a great way for her to exact revenge on me, she knew what shift I was on and when I was on nights she used to wait till I'd had chance to be asleep for a couple of hours, then go to a friend across the road and ring her own phone and leave it going till all the dogs howled. I didn't realise she was the culprit at first, though it did seem strange to be happening at more or less the same time every day. I'd changed shifts with one of the lads at work so didn't need to sleep that day but still closed me curtains as usual and then watched to see what would happen. Sure enough at the usual time she left the house and went across to the woman's house across the road, a few minutes later the phone rang and the dogs started howling, they made the mistake of looking out of the window phone in hand and laughing. I felt sorry for the dogs being whipped into frenzy day after day. I just went and slept at my mums when I was on nights after that till she got over herself. Eventually we managed to pass the time of day in a civil manner, so were on speaking terms by the time they left to live at his mum's house as she'd passed away.

Globe Trotter

One of the darts teams I played for was the Miners Club, which was a friendly club on the whole. One of the ladies used to get upset if anyone else sat where she wanted to sit, I was of the opinion first come first served so am afraid I upset her on a fairly regular basis so to be fair she wasn't really very keen on me. When she retired she immigrated to Canada as her daughter and grandchildren lived there and they were sponsoring her, which made it possible. Of course we had a farewell party for her which was very nice and everyone said they would keep in touch, she left her daughters address with us until such time as she had her own. She wrote to one of the ladies that she had been close to for many years and she brought it in to let us read, this happened a few times and each time she sounded more and more desperate for news of home. Her friend it turned out wasn't much of a writer and hadn't replied to any of her letters! I felt a bit sorry for her and took it upon myself to write to her, not really expecting to hear back as I wasn't her most favourite person. I always enjoyed corresponding so wrote her newsy letters to try and stave off some of her homesickness. We ended up being better friends as pen pals than we had as team members.

It all sounded very lovely and I'd said rather wistfully I suppose that I should like to see Canada one day, I was amazed when she invited me to come for a holiday, given the relationship we had before she went. Anyway I saved up hard and eventually went. I'm not very thrilled about flying so an eleven-hour flight all on my own was a bit daunting to say the least. Fortunately I was sat with a very nice couple that were friendly and chatty and the time passed reasonably quickly. My destination was Ottawa and there wasn't a direct flight to that airport so I had to get on another plane for the last part of the journey. My jaw dropped when I saw what I had to get on it looked like a toy compared to what I'd just got off. There was only enough seats for eight passengers, it didn't take long but I was petrified for every single moment of the flight, my legs had completely gone to jelly by the time I arrived.

Trish didn't drive but one of her neighbours in the senior's apartments she lived in brought her to pick me up, a very nice man. Unfortunately he fancied Trish and she led him round by the nose to get him to do stuff for her and was nice to him when it suited.

I hadn't realised how hot and humid it would be, spent most of my time trying to keep cool, she didn't have air conditioning as she suffered from asthma and it didn't agree with her. She did have a little balcony which was a godsend in the night as I was able to have the full length doors wide open and a fan facing across my bed as well as a ceiling fan, that way I managed to get a bit of sleep. In the daytime we went in a lot of malls, as they were fully air-conditioned, I've never enjoyed shopping but must say I didn't mind putting up with it so I could breath.

She laughed when she saw all the clothes I'd brought, especially the trousers, and informed me I'd spend most of my time in shorts. I didn't really believe her and given I'm not exactly the right shape for shorts thought it was a load of rubbish.

The first night we went out to play darts I found out how right she was, I was there looking the picture of sartorial elegance in my nicely pressed trousers, smart shirt and highly polished shoes, everyone else men and woman alike were in shorts and t-shirts and sandals. They were in all shapes and sizes as well so I didn't need to be too worried about what I'd look like when I joined them the next time. Everyone was very friendly and I was invited to play in their teams with them it was all very loose and relaxed. She'd been telling them all about me apparently and even had a lesbian lined up to meet me, which surprised me I must say. The woman she introduced me to was a native North American so that was quite exotic and different as far as I was concerned. What was strange was as soon as Trish saw that we were getting on well she started backtracking and being less than friendly about her. I thought that was really strange, why bother introducing us in the first place?

I had thought I may hire a car whilst I was there, but couldn't get my head round the driving on the wrong side of the road so thought I'd stick with public transport. So we went to Quebec by coach and stayed overnight in a nice hotel, that was a beautiful place. Another trip took us by train to Torronto for an overnight stay on the way to Niagra, It was quite funny when we went out for the evening as nearly all the pubs and bars were Irish, I thought I'd time travelled to Ireland. We went for something to eat on the way back to the hotel and I ordered a club sandwich it was huge, could have kept me going for a week if I could have managed it all. The next day we went down to the bay and there was a beautiful triple mast schooner there so we went for the trip round the harbour, she didn't tell me till it set of that she couldn't stand boats and got sick on them, then moaned the whole time, I could have willingly strangled her it only lasted an hour so she could have had a coffee at the pretty little café on the bay. I enjoyed the trip in spite of her moaning I love anything to do with boats and water.

We carried on to Niagara by train in the afternoon, we picked up a taxi to the hotel and I was a bit disappointed by Niagara itself as we drove through, I had this romantic image in my head from various films and I felt like I was being driven through a very tatty version of Blackpool's Golden Mile, without the illuminations. The little hotel we stayed at was lovely everything was just right; we had a nice meal and an early night, to be ready for the Falls the next day. I was up very early and whilst Trish was getting ready had a lovely swim in the pool, which I had all to myself a real joy.

Off we went to the Falls I was really excited but did wonder about Trish and whether she would get on "The Maid of the Mist". Apparently it was only triple- mast schooners that made her ill, not little boats that bumped about like corks in the wash of the falls! It was great; having something that powerful right above you is awesome. Also the added bonus was the noise not a moan could be heard. I also had a go on a rickety cable car that went across a raging torrent a bit further down from the falls, Trish didn't join me on that. I saw a Mountie but was a bit disappointed as there was only the one and it was a lady, obviously just there for the tourists but all in all a lovely day. We popped back in the evening to see the Falls illuminated but I preferred it in its natural state. Back to Ottawa the next day tired but happy.

I must say I enjoyed my holiday immensely and people were very friendly, as well as the darts nights I was invited to a few barbeques which were a bit different to the ones we have as the weather was guaranteed. We went to stay at Trish's daughters for a couple of days, her grandsons were delightful and we got on really well.

They used to watch Coronation street only about six months behind us, it was their Sunday morning viewing so I left them to it and was playing in the garden with the kids when they suddenly shouted me in, It was the news of Princess Diane's death which was a shock, such a lovely vibrant young woman. We were going to one of the big lakes that day but because of the death we were unable to access it as some dignitary had the roads cordoned off and were obviously involved in the royal family in some way. So a bit like everyone knowing where they were when John Kennedy died, I'll always know where I was at the moment Diane was killed.

In Ottawa they have houses of parliament that are replicas of ours, when we went to see it we suddenly found ourselves being addressed by Queen Victoria from a balcony, she was very good and looked very like the images I've seen. We went back there to sign the condolence book for Diane but the queue was horrendous and I struggled with the heat and humidity so we had to give in.

On the last day before I came home we were invited to a party at a couples house, they were British but had been there for years. They had a beautiful home and the huge basement had been made into a replica of an English pub with many dartboards and real British beer. A lot of our touring darts players used to visit them there and occasionally stay; they had their photos mounted all over the room. Who should turn up that afternoon but Dusty, the Native American that Trish introduced me to then tried to keep me separated from! She had been supposed to pick me up one day to go somewhere and let me down which had incensed Trish and said it proved what a waste of space she was. I wasn't thrilled about being let down but it wasn't the end of the world. Anyway at some stage during the party she apologised and gave me her phone number and asked if I would ring her from the airport. I did once I was in the departure lounge as I had about an hour to kill. She asked if she could write to me so I gave her my address as I've always enjoyed letter writing, deep down I didn't really expect to hear from her but it was all very flattering and I'd nothing to lose.

Different Team

At some stage I changed my darts team and went to play for the Football I can't remember why. There I met Anne who was to become a great pal and sturdy friend. When we first got chatting I nearly upset her quite by accident, she has an occasional stutter that only comes out under stress or when she's excited, unfortunately I'm one of those people who picks up other peoples accents or impediments without even realising I'm doing it. She thought I was taking the piss! I wasn't so there nearly wasn't a friendship in the first place.

She was to be my straight mate and me her butch buddy, we had many laughs along the way and often had to tell people we were just pals as they couldn't believe two such different people could get on so well without anything going on.

I started subscribing to darts world and it opened a whole new part to my life as that's when I found out how to go to all the different darts venues up and down the country. I mentioned it at darts but said I didn't fancy going on my own, not as brave as I thought I was. Anne jumped at the chance and said she'd like to come, I said wouldn't her husband object to her going away with a lesbian? Apparently not and funnily enough the first venue we were going to attend was at the Isle of Man and he used to go there every year for the TT races, as he loved his motorbike so everyone was happy. We had a brilliant time, entered all the competitions, didn't get very far but we tried, It was exciting meeting all the top darts players that we'd only ever seen playing on the television shows. With one exception, I'd met and played against Cliff Lazerenko in London and he was really nice to me at the time.

When I saw him there I went to introduce myself to him and say I'd met him before and he stopped me in my tracks by remembering me, even my name! I was impressed, as he must meet thousands of people in his travels.

After the initial visit to the I-O-M, we made it our business to book up for every year and also went to other places where they had competitions on holiday camps one of which was Cleethorpes which was a placed I'd lived for a little while as a child so a trip down memory lane as well as another fun weekend.

All in all I was really enjoying my life, working hard and playing hard as well. Also I was getting lots of beautiful love letters from Dusty in Canada. I was amazed, as she didn't look like the type to write soppy letters and poetry, that's a bit judgemental I suppose, as I probably don't look the type either. Anyway I was thoroughly enjoying being the recipient. I fell in love with the letters but never ever dreamt we meet again so it made it all the more poignant.

My nanas birthday was the sixth of December and my mum and I always went to see her, to celebrate it with her. At the same time my mum used to help her write her Christmas cards as her arthritis hampered her from doing it herself. I must have been there nearly every time this happened for most of it but all of a sudden I heard my mum say "what do you want me to write on Viv and Frank's card?" I hadn't realised they would have her address and I was really excited. She was ten when I was born and I was the first baby in the family after her so we had a bond but had lost track of each other over the years. I wrote to her straight away and enclosed it in a very early Christmas card. I didn't have to wait long for a reply and it dropped through my letterbox with a thump, a big manila envelope containing a very long letter various photographs of her large and lovely family, one of which was a wedding group which she had outlined with tracing paper and numbered everyone, then named them all twenty-one relatives some of whom were completely new to me. I was thrilled to bits. This was to start years of long lovely letters all written on A- four sheets as we both seemed to have lots to say for ourselves and normal writing pads wouldn't accommodate our verbosity. It was exciting to catch up on all the years we had lost, we worked it out to thirty-four. Viv was profoundly deaf so our long chatty letters would have been someone else's telephone calls but you can't savour them and reread them, which we did till we got used to each other again. I was longing to see her and the rest of the family but hadn't managed to broach the fact that I was gay to her a bit cowardly I suppose but it's not something that pops up in a conversational letter unless you are trying to make an issue of it and I wasn't. Nevertheless when she invited me to Basingstoke I was worried that I'd be rejected. My pal Ann came with me and kept me boosted on the drive down there, telling me she wouldn't be able to do anything else but love me, a bit over the top but it helped. When we arrived I was enfolded in a giant bear hug and told I hadn't changed a bit and she would have recognised me anywhere. What a relief, nothing was said about my 'gayness' until a long way down the line and it wasn't a problem. I don't think it would have mattered if I had two heads we loved each other and that was that, of course the other bond was that she had always loved my nana dearly. So we had a lovely visit and Ann was adopted as well, Ann chose to call her Aunty Viv. Whilst we were their all her children bobbed in and out at various times, it was hard to keep track of everyone, I knew the two oldest sons as I'd babysat for them when I was ten but hadn't met the other boy and two girls. Then there were all the grandchildren I was dizzy by the time it finished. The most loving family I have ever met.

So from then on there were lots of visits both ways and of course our very long weekly letters, you'd think we would have run out of things to say but there were thirty-four long years of catching up to be done. Viv was a very good decorator and she came and stayed with me and decorated my living room for me but with much patience showed me how to do it. We discovered a wallpaper factory in Chorley where you could buy slightly damaged paper for peanuts, we had a ball selecting loads for her to take home, she had nearly enough to do her home for a few years and half the estate she lived in, it was a good job I was driving her back she'd never got on a train with it! Another time she came and helped me decorate my mums bedroom, hall and landing. It was a big job but very satisfying when we'd finished it all. My mum drove her mad as she could talk the hind leg off a donkey, much worse than me, but she kept stopping our progress with all the chat so Viv decided to ignore her and just get on with it, it was hilarious as my mum was trotting around behind chattering away and Viv was oblivious to it all, my mum on the other hand was quite convinced that all her pearls of wisdom were being heeded as Viv wore a hearing aid, but it was to allow her to hear her own voice and modulate her tone, just couldn't get my mum to grasp that so she spent a lot of time talking to herself.

Visitor from Hell

Well my correspondence with Dusty in Canada carried on and was getting more and more intimate by the letter. I also received lots of photos of her daughter and granddaughter and felt like I was being drawn into her life. So when she suggested coming over for a holiday I was thrilled to bits and looking forward to the time immensely.

In the meantime I had been visiting my friend Rene who lived not far from the Lake District. She hadn't been too well so I was trying to give her a bit of company. She had a friend she used to visit called Joan and I got to know her quite well, she was about my mums age and a right old character, very butch smoked like a trooper and said (it how it was), which I liked. She told me lots of tales from her younger days and we found there were a few parallels like the fact we both used to be clippies on the buses though separated by many years there was still plenty of common ground. She was in a ladies football team during the war years and had plenty of yarns to tell about that time in her life and was thrilled that the team had a book published about them called 'A League Of Their Own', a good part of it was dedicated to Joan and at a later date I was to meet the author. She also enjoyed hearing about my exploits and I used to make her laugh, she lived in an old manor house in a village called Yealand Conyers, it sounds quite grand but she was in a tiny room right at the top which had obviously once been the servant's quarters. The staircase was very narrow and steep and it nearly killed me getting up there, but she loved it as the views across the countryside were lovely and many different birds used to feed off her windowsill and were very tame with her. Rene ended up getting a bit jealous of our friendship, though she wasn't left out in any way she just didn't like sharing. Anyway I ended up writing to Joan as well as Rene, I had written to Rene for years but it was hit and miss if you had a reply and always scrawled in haste, though why I don't know it wasn't as if she was doing much. I came to the conclusion that she loved having a chatty letter sent to her but wasn't too thrilled at having to write one back, like chalk and cheese Joan wrote lovely letters and even though she didn't move out of her room much used to make them newsy and funny.

Eventually the fags took their toll on Joan and she ended up in Christie's cancer hospital in Manchester with throat cancer. Fortunately it wasn't far from where I worked and I was able to visit her regularly as it was a bit too far for her other friends to come. She still remained cheerful through her trials and tribulations even though she had to wear a dreadful lead mask for her treatment. I was thrilled when she was given the all clear and the cancer had abated.

A month or so after the good news I went to see her and was shocked to see she could hardly move with very swollen ankles, she was getting some medication for it but not much was happening to help. The next thing I had a phone call from Rene to say Joan had been rushed into hospital. I couldn't get off work for a few days but sent her a get-well card and wrote her a comical poem in with the letter. She had passed away before she got it. The reason I'm mentioning all this is she was looking forward to meeting my friend from Canada as much as I was and blow me wasn't it to be Joan's funeral to be the day after Dusty arrived. I wouldn't have missed going to say farewell to my pal but thought if Dusty didn't want to come she could rest up and get over her jet lag.

I went to meet her at Manchester airport full of excitement, butterflies in the tummy the whole gamut of different feelings. I was straining my eyes looking for her so it was a real shock to my system when this huge woman in a bright yellow cagoule presented herself to me! I'm not often stuck for words but I was then, she was nothing at all like my memory of her I was shocked talk about rose coloured spectacles. I quickly gathered myself together and set about greeting her and getting her home.

I suppose the romantic in me had visions of us floating across the airport with open arms and eyes full of love and hurling ourselves into a passionate clinch, If she'd have done any hurling or clinching I would have been unconscious! When we got home it was a bit uncomfortable but I didn't want to be unkind or spoil her holiday and I don't usually judge a book by its cover so thought maybe everything would work out in the end. I explained about Joan's funeral and she insisted in coming, really I didn't want her to but what could I say? It was a nightmare she was dog rough and really coarse and common, my toes were curling up in my shoes every time she opened her mouth I was frightened what would come out of it. I did meet Joan's family and they were lovely, in the meantime the card and letter with the poem that I'd sent to the hospital found its way back to me and I showed it to her sister who asked me to read it out loud as Joan used to tell them about my letters and they thought she would have liked me to read them. It was quite emotional but I was glad I was able to do that for them.

I thought I would at least try and make her holiday memorable for her, it wasn't her fault that I was so fickle as to be shocked she didn't match up to her beautiful love letters. Well that was my intention but as the saying goes the road to hell is full of good intentions.

When she eventually got up the next day which was early afternoon (I put it down to jet lag), we went off to the local market and shops which she seemed quite excited about, I've never been keen on shopping but each to their own. I stocked up with lots of cooked meats and treats for picnics planning to take her off and show her some of our beautiful countryside especially the Lake District thinking she'd enjoy the comparison of our lakes to the wonderful ones in Canada. When we came home I cooked our evening meal and she was amazed at the size of the dinner I gave her but nevertheless managed to eat every morsel. We had a quiet night in just watching the telly and chatting in general. I was dreading bedtime coming round in case she recovered enough from her journey that she expected me to make love to her! She had said that she would prefer to sleep in the spare room when she arrived so I supposed I should be thankful for small mercies. We went to bed I gave her time to settle in before going up washing cups and faffing around at anything rather than go up and see which bed she had deposited herself in! It was with relief that I found my bed empty! Very short lived as soon as I switched the light out she came bouncing in waiting to be serviced, it was dreadful if I'd been a man I wouldn't have been able to oblige but not having that problem I had to go through the motions. I'm glad to say when it was over and done with she went back to her own room. I felt a bit like a prostitute must feel only without the payment to make it worthwhile.

The next day I was up bright and early, the weather was lovely so thought I would start preparing our picnic ready to go to the lakes. Opened the fridge and thought I was losing my mind, there was hardly anything there, all the cooked meat I'd bought the day before was gone which included a pound of ham, half a pound of beef, half a pound of lunch tongue a pork pie and a quiche. It's not often I'm stuck for words but I was that morning. I tried to wake her up to go for our day out (without the picnic) but she wasn't having in it she just kept turning over and going back to sleep so I gave up.

That was to set the pattern she didn't want to get up till the afternoon and ate me out of house and home. When I'd tried to tackle her about the missing food she said she was my guest and it was very rude of me to ask her about what she'd used and thought it was there for her anyway. I was fuming but it wasn't as if I could throw her out when she'd travelled all that way.

I took her to meet my mum thought I'd get it out of the way and whilst I was there borrowed some of mum's sleeping pills. No, I wasn't considering bumping her off they were for me so I could be unconscious when she decided to pay me nocturnal visits as I found out she didn't understand what no meant.

Of course I had to take her with me when I went to play darts, I was dreading it as I'd been so excited about her coming and they'd all been thrilled for me as I'd been waxing lyrical about her for months. It was a nightmare she spent the evening bumming drinks off anyone who spoke to her, they were all trying to be nice for my benefit. When she wasn't doing that she was chatting them up and most of them were straight ladies. It was a long evening, which I spent most of trotting behind her apologising. A couple of friends took pity on me and invited us back to their home for drinks as they lived opposite the pub we had been playing at. I jumped at the chance anything rather than go home with her. Things didn't seem too bad they were nice lasses and quite happy to overlook her performance in the pub and were interested to hear a bit about Canada as one of them had a son who was going there to play ice-hockey. My mouth dropped open when she sat in the middle of their living room floor and gave a blow-by-blow account of what happened between us in the bedroom! I could hardly believe my ears, I was furious and big as she was I managed to drag her up of the floor and frogmarch her home. How I stopped myself from doing her an injury I'll never know.

After that I just settled to shovelling food down her throat and praying for the time to pass. In the middle of her three week stay she announced she was going to Paisley in Scotland to see a friend who used to live in Canada, I was jubilant and hoping she wouldn't bother to come back. I had a whole week to myself what bliss.

When she did return she did nothing but carp about her friends so I can only assume she treated them much the same as she did me and they didn't like it either. She wanted to go to flea markets all the time or car boot sales and she bought loads of real tatty stuff, which I couldn't believe she wanted to take back with her, she bought so much she had to buy another suitcase to accommodate it all and it was a large one. I was also horrified to find out she'd been shoplifting, what a complete horror she was. When I took her to the airport for her journey home they wanted fifty pounds from her to pay for the excess baggage and she only tried to get me to pay for it, the stuff she had wasn't worth more than a tenner it was all rubbish. I cried when she went through passport control but it was tears of joy to see the back of her.

When I got home I went to sort the spare room out, change the bedding and give it a general clean up. I moved the bed out to hoover and found stacks of food wrappings obviously from her all night eating jags I couldn't believe she'd managed to stuff so much in on top of what she had in the daytime. Another episode of my life very gladly over and done with I was quite pleased to get back to work and try and forget I'd had the visit. Therefore I was astounded when I started getting love letters again, I couldn't believe the cheek of it, especially as my friend in Canada had already told me she was telling people I never took her anywhere, If she'd have got out of bed now and again I would have! I just ignored her and eventually she gave up I'm pleased to say.

Back To Normal

I carried along quite happily with my darts and trips to the sing-along pub; I was enjoying my life and always seemed to have a good crowd of friends around me especially my mate who used to sing for us. He also brought his pals along with him often and we all got on very well and had a laugh. So you can imagine my confusion when the wife of one of his mates turned up at my place of work one night. She had asked me where I worked but I thought it was just showing an interest especially as I wasn't far from Manchester United Football Club, people quite often were interested in that.

Well it wasn't the location she was interested in and she soon made that clear. I was amazed but very available being footloose and fancy free, though I did draw the line at doing anything about it whilst at work, tempting as it was. So she used to pop down to see me once a week and we had some lovely afternoons, I suppose I was very flattered as she lived about thirty miles away but must have thought it was worth the effort.

Round about this time Maggie tried to pop back into my life, she turned up at my door saying she'd come to get her voting card, as a thin excuse that must be the winner, it was the sixth of May so the actual voting day, I didn't let her in but offered to drive her to the polling station as I was going anyway but only on condition that she voted the same as me, she did. Afterwards we went to have a drink in a nearby pub and she filled me in with what she'd been doing. I knew most of it anyway as there was always someone ready to let me know what was happening even though I wasn't interested. The upshot was she'd left the home for battered wives to move in with a girl, it hadn't worked out so she'd gone back to the battered wives home, they must have been a gullible lot there even worse than me. She said she missed the nights out at the Oddy's (sing along pub), so I said there was nothing to stop her going, definitely not me, so she started turning up. I had no reason to be unfriendly as she wasn't my problem anymore so we probably got on better in that period of time than we ever had. She had to be in by a certain time at the home and often tried to miss the bus in the hope that she'd be able to stay with me but I kept my eye on the time and walked her to the bus stop. She did miss it on one occasion but a couple of my friends stepped in and gave her a lift.

I don't know how she managed it but she got a council flat just up the road from The Oddy's. It was very nice and I was glad to see Daniel settled again. As time went by she managed to swap the flat for a house across the road from me, again I don't know how she did it but there she was nearly opposite me. I did help her move in and we held a decorating party, not much painting but plenty of drinking ensued. The good thing was Daniel could come and see me whenever he felt like it, which was nice. He was with me one day when Maggie rang up in a panic to say the house was on fire! We shot over there and while Daniel calmed her down and got her out I put the fire out. She'd put some bacon under the grill and fallen asleep so it could have been worse and definitely looked bad with all the black smoke, I'd put it out by the time the fire brigade arrived and got a telling off for doing it. She had only had the cooker installed the day before it was lucky it was insured.

Eventually she realised we were never going to become a couple again and said if I wasn't interested she would move to Yorkshire where her eldest daughter had gone, so she did though we remained friends and I did go over to see her new council house when she'd settled in.

Millennium

We were galloping towards the millennium and there seemed to be much excitement about it, what everyone was going to be doing as it started. Would all the computers in the world have a problem and throw everyone into utter confusion? For my part I can't say I was very interested, as far as I was concerned it was just another date on the calendar and as for making plans I knew from a long way before I was to be working the nightshift over the whole holiday so wasn't bothered in the least. My curiosity did go up a notch when my boss suddenly offered to do my night shift on New Year's Eve! He never worked on any of the bank holidays so there had to be an ulterior motive, I said thank you for the offer but I'm quite happy to stick with my own shift, he looked crestfallen. I was to find out much later that Unilever like a lot of other big company's was to pay silly wages to their top dogs to be on duty in case the computers went haywire on the night and it was to encompass all staff that worked for Unilever even the lowly little basic wage security guards! What joy! The little folk were to come out on top for once I was all but doing a jig, it wasn't just for the one night either but the whole holiday, I was paid thousands just for doing my very ordinary job! The other up side of it was the wonderful firework displays I got to see being just across from Manchester United's Old Trafford and a stone's throw from Manchester city centre, I think I had the best seat in the house. I also had permission to take a television into work so could see what was happening around the world. The extra money was to have a knock on effect to do with my pension another plus.

I already knew that I was going to be redundant in the New Year, it was on offer for voluntary redundancy and I had decided to take them up on it so it was just a case of waiting for the date to come through.

Part of our job was to keep a log of our activities especially when on night -shift, unless something was very wrong there obviously wouldn't be an awful lot to report. Most of us would just put the time and the fact that we did a patrol and all was secure or quiet. We did check calls with another site every two hours to make sure we were all safe that would be logged in and so on, nothing to make a song and dance about. Except one of the chaps wrote every single detail he could think of, what could be written in a sentence became a chapter. The sheets we used for logs were massive if I stretched it out I could fill half a page leaving gaps in between, John managed to fill about three sheets in with no trouble at all. So I thought I'd have a bit of fun with him. The factory was partially an old mill with lots of antiquated equipment which nevertheless still functioned, it could be quite scary till you got used to it, there were paddles banging in big hoppers, sounds like a giant sighing and plenty of creaks and groans that could fire any ones imagination. The factory workers used to clock off at ten pm and that's when our main activity of the evening started for the security guard on duty. You would go round and lock all doors inside and out switch off all the lights before handing over to the next guard who would start at eleven pm. That's what I would write but of course John would mention every single door and every light switch! When he arrived on this particular night I was still writing in the log so I could keep my face averted from him. I said "I've just had a strange experience whilst locking up but I'm not going to put it in the log as everyone will take the Mickey out of me". Of course his curiosity was piqued and he wanted to know what had happened. So I told him when I'd arrived on the third floor I saw a man walking out through the door to the stairwell on the other side of the building, he was in his fifties, short of stature and in need of a shave, salt and pepper hair and was wearing a brown overall, which made me follow him as we don't have that colour overall in the company, just white or navy blue! When I got to the stairwell I searched up and down and called out but there was no response and no trace whatsoever, bemused I retraced my steps and as I did I realised he'd gone through the doors without actually opening them! "So you can see why I'm not putting that in the log, no one would believe me!" I said. John had gone very white, his eyes were wide with disbelief but is was a very old factory and I'm sure there must have been stories like that before so I wished him a cheery goodnight and went home.

When I arrived the next day to start my shift at three pm it was to find John already there before me, I'd forgotten it was payday and that was why he was there. The occupants of the lodge, my boss, a factory foreman, weighbridge operator and a lorry driver were all agog to hear the story straight from the horse's mouth! I'd been going to tell everyone it was a joke but decided that discretion was the better part of valour when confronted with them all so went ahead and described the apparition to them! The foreman had worked there for twenty five years and mentioned the maintenance men used to wear brown overalls he said "that would be Joe Palowski, he fell out of the third story window fifteen years ago and injured his back so badly that he was unable to return to work and died of his injuries six months later!" Spooky, how could I confess to making it all up with all that evidence to back me up, then again maybe I did see it after all, this did happen a little earlier in my story and it was Halloween! To this day they may believe that Joe walks the third floor checking the machinery.

I'd only done it for fun to try and shake him out of the habit of writing every single thing down. When they'd all left I looked in the log and sure enough he'd written everything down that I'd told him as best as he could with the tag line being " I must say what she said has me shitting myself!"

Occasionally a couple of the young men from the test bakery came in to bake some special batches of bread to be ready for visitors arriving first thing in the morning, so of course they had to come in the night to do it. I found it highly amusing that these young men asked me to escort them to the test bakery (on the third floor of the old building) as they were nervous, then when they'd finished and wanted to go home they rang for me to come and get them, I don't know what they thought I could actually do if we were confronted with a ghost!

I was given my leaving date for the redundancy, it was the end of March, I had quite a bit of annual leave to use up so decided to go to Scotland as I'd never been except for one flying visit to Glasgow to do a quiz show in the BBC studios there. Maggie had gone to Edinburgh University and had a student flat and had invited me so I took advantage of the offer. The flat was really lovely and in the summer was let out to tourists as it was nearly on the Royal Mile and nestled beneath Arthur's Seat. It fascinated me the way she always landed on her feet no matter what. Anyway after doing the usual touristy things round Edinburgh I decided on a bit of a tour which I enjoyed immensely the scenery is lovely. I drove up one side as far as Loch Ness and then we made our way down the other side visiting Oban as my nana had said she went there and loved it and also stayed at Fort William a lovely little tour. Then a mad dash back to get my redundancy pay, which was exciting, as I'd never, had that much money all in one go.

I decided to give myself a few weeks off whilst deciding what to do next. My present to my mum for Christmas was an IOU to fully decorate and carpet her living room so that was a good time to get on with it. I moved her into my house so I could get on with it uninterrupted which worked very well as the council had decided to put new central heating in mine so mum was there to supervise that.

I also decided to go back to Canada for another visit; Trish who I stayed with had been back for a visit and invited me to go again so I thought why not. Before I went I thought about it a lot and decided I would like to work as a Carer, given I wasn't able to look after my nana I would try and look after other peoples. So I enrolled in a short course at college to learn about moving and handling, how to use hoists and other equipment.

Of I went to Canada, feeling like quite the globe-trotter, we wasn't going to be dashing round the country sightseeing this time just a more restful holiday, it was much too hot for rushing around anyway. Trish had seen Dusty and someone had told her I was coming so she was making noises that she would like to see me again, Trish sent her off with a flea in her ear. What transpired was quite amusing and could only happen to me. We went to the bar Trish usually played darts in and all was well, whilst she was playing her game I went to the toilet and the door got jammed! Try as I might I couldn't get out, I knew no-one would hear if I shouted so just decided to wait till the next person came in and ask for help. I'd been there about ten minutes and someone came in I shouted out and explained what had happened and a hand came over the top of the door and a lot of pushing and shoving ensued from the other side, all of a sudden it gave way, what a relief but a short lived one as who should be pushing herself through my means of escape but Dusty! I was trapped and from gasping out thanks to what I thought would be a stranger I ended up having a row with my nightmare visitor. I couldn't get out of there quick enough, she must have a short- term memory as she was saying how she cared for me and how she'd missed me, I fled. Trish and I giggled about it when we got back to her flat but it wasn't a happy experience and of all the people in the bar it had to be her coming to my rescue!

Back home I settled myself down to looking for a job as a Carer, I registered with an agency that did home visits to get a bit of grounding but it wasn't for me, too hit and miss as to whether you got any clients, new carers tended to get the more difficult clients which wasn't a good idea if you were inexperienced. I managed to get a position in a nursing home near where I lived and off I went full of enthusiasm expecting to be helping lovely little old ladies to get dressed and serving their meals and anything else they needed. When I took my rose-tinted glasses off I came to earth with a bang, I'd been put on a 'locked in' dementia ward with eight ladies and two men in varying stages of the complaint. I was terrified and didn't think I would be able to cope with it, although they had all the other ailments that usually come with age because of the dementia they didn't take any notice of aches and pains and when you was trying to help them get dressed or washed they would be off like greyhounds. I didn't think I was going to be able to do this, I watched in horror at the way some of the carers were feeding the ladies that couldn't feed themselves, ramming great spoons full in their mouths before they swallowed what was already there. While the ones that could were mainly playing with the food and throwing it about, I've always had a tickly stomach and found myself heaving for most of the first few days especially when I realised that changing grown up nappies were involved not to mention stripping all the soiled beds. To cut a very long story short I found I was good at it when I got over myself and had a lot more patience than the youngsters that worked there. I ended up looking after two ladies who were classed as 'heavies' because they couldn't move or do anything for themselves, one could move her arms and flailed them about the whole time you was trying to feed her and I got many a crack round the head because I didn't duck fast enough. The other lady could only move one arm and didn't speak except to make funny shrieking noises, I was to fall in love with her, she was such a sweetheart, once I'd gained her trust and fed her like a human being and talked to her all the time she was a lot calmer. I had a look in her records and tried to find out the sort of things she used to like, dancing was one thing so that didn't help but when her daughter came she seemed amazed that I was bothering to ask anything and was a bit standoffish but I did find she used to like going to sing along pubs a thing I enjoyed as well. So I asked if it was alright for me to bring a music centre in, someone had given me one and I didn't use it, I scoured around and found a lot of sing along records Max Bygraves, Val Doonican and the like. The youngsters were looking at me like I was bonkers when I set it all up but it was a lovely and complete success. Most of the other patients came in the lounge and listened some even danced around, my lady clapped her hand on my hand and smiled the whole way through, she was in time to the music so I knew she was getting it.

Something as simple as that and a bit of thought made all the difference. The company gave me some money to get some things to keep them entertained, I got penny whistles, drums and tambourines anything that they could join in with and it was great. So from being horrified at the job in the first place I found myself looking forward to being there. The best bit for me was when we had a Halloween party, I was in another room helping with the food and one of the carers ran in and said "Caroline's asking for you", I said "don't be daft she can't speak" apparently she was shouting my name, I rushed in and there she was shouting Andy over and over again when I got there she gave a great big chuckle and tried to hug me with her one good arm. Next day she started saying her daughter's name and when she came to visit I told her and she cried, she said " about three years before her mum had looked round the room they were in and said it's no good talking to anyone in here I won't bother anymore and that was the last time she'd spoken". I was thrilled to bits that she'd changed her mind.

Not long after that my little world came crashing down as I injured my back, unfortunately it was while trying to put Caroline to bed. The hoist wouldn't fit in her room, not many of the others either so the senior nurse and I were halfway to putting her to bed when my back went, and we had to lower her to the floor then with a superhuman effort get her up to the bed. I went to work the next day but had to give up and go home it was useless and that was the last time I worked.

I still went in to visit Caroline whilst I was on sick and tried to make it at meal times so I could feed her but in the end I was so upset by her decline that I had to stop going. Shortly after her family moved Caroline to another home but she passed away not long after.

The care home offered me a job as entertainments officer but unfortunately I was so up and down with my back injury I couldn't manage it, I'd be alright for a couple of days then barley capable of movement for the next few days.

I was lucky I had some very good friends around me when things were at their worst so I got through the worst part with support.

Sorrow

In the ups and downs of life the start of the next year was definitely a down! I used to go to Fleetwood every three weeks to see my nana and Uncle Harry, collect their laundry, do the shopping, anything that I could to make their lives easier. My uncle had a dreadful smokers cough and had it for years but no amount of coaxing or nagging could get him to see a doctor, they made him fearful. So when he rang me to say he wasn't well and needed help I knew it was going to be bad, but still had to bully him saying if he wouldn't have a doctor when I came up there would be nothing I could do, he said yes straight away so it was with much trepidation I drove up there. He said he would have the doctor but not till the next day, as he needed help with having a wash, so that was the deal. I thought he was stalling but when I got him stripped off in the living room near the fire my heart was breaking. I had seen pictures of the poor people of Belsen concentration camp and he looked just like them. My hand could nearly span the top of his leg, he had been wearing so many layers of clothes that no-one could know and my poor little scarecrow of an uncle had been lifting my nana in and out of bed to use the commode all this time. I also found out that he had never slept in his bed for years as he was frightened he wouldn't wake up for his mum, he used to muss it up a bit so I wouldn't know when I collected his bedding and changed it for him, so I'd been washing clean bedding for years as well.

The doctor came in the morning and that was the first time he'd got in the bed, the doctor was visibly shocked at his condition. He sent us straight to the hospital for an X-ray and we had barely been back half an hour when the doctor was knocking on the door, it was lung cancer he was riddled with it but he outright refused any treatment whatsoever. I won't go into a load of gruelling details but he was given a full time care package and there was someone there through the night for him, he still wouldn't go to bed as he'd sat up for so long it was painful to lie down. The carers weren't allowed to see to my nana so I was there most of the time, she had a couple that came in to wash her in the day but no night care. I had to go home for a hospital appointment for my back and would be going back the next day but one of the carers I'd become very friendly with rang me to say she'd had to get an ambulance for him and he was in hospital in Blackpool he'd heard my nana shout his name, jumped up out of a sleep and fallen and banged his head on the sideboard. Because he was bleeding she was duty bound to get an ambulance. As a favour to me she said she would stay with my nana till the morning carer came in. I knew it would be the end, he had such a fear of hospitals. My mum was in denial and didn't want to believe how bad he was so wouldn't come with me even though I'd spoken to the hospital and they weren't holding out any hope. It was a horrible stressful drive and when I arrived at my nana's it was to find her alone as the daytime carer had to leave, she didn't know she was alone which was a blessing. Unfortunately I was stuck as I couldn't leave her and the hospital kept ringing me saying I needed to get there. I rang my neighbour up in Manchester who very kindly went and brought my mum to me, she had no sooner arrived when my cousin came to stay with my nana whilst we got to the hospital.

He was lying there looking dead already which to be honest I think he was, he had an oxygen mask on and there was no response at all. We had barely been there an hour when my mum was champing at the bit to get back to my nana (not that she'd been in a hurry to get there in the first place), I got hold of a senior nurse and asked her if she knew how long he would be with us? She said not long and I explained the situation with my nana and mum, she came back to the bed with me, drew the curtains round us and removed the oxygen mask and that was that, he went. It was stark I'd worshipped him all my life, as he had no children he'd spoilt me rotten the only father figure I'd ever known. I didn't get chance to even have a weep because reality had hit home with my mum at long last and she went to bits weeping and wailing for both of us.

Trying to tell my nana was awful, initially she said "but he's so young" he was seventy-nine and her first born, she was ninety-seven so to her he was young. Unfortunately for us her short-term memory wasn't so good so it was a bit like ground hog day, as we had to keep telling her over and over again which was awful for all of us. She couldn't understand why he didn't come in to kiss her goodnight and when she wanted anything cries of Harry rang round the house and she was doomed to disappointment each time it was me that turned up. She only took it on board the day of the funeral when everyone was milling around and making a fuss of her. Well that was the beginning of the end once Uncle Harry had gone she just gave up and let herself drift away from us to go and be with him, she passed away peacefully in her sleep forty eight days after he died. My two most loved, favourite people in the world all gone.

On the day of my nanas funeral I completely broke down, all the crying I'd been unable to do came flooding out in one fell swoop. I couldn't really hear the service; I could barely see the coffin although I was on the front row. All of a sudden in the midst of all my grief I heard a slight giggle and a lot of rustling as people turned round and craned their necks to see something. It was a little terrier marching straight up the centre of the isle looking very purposeful, he went straight to the stand the coffin was on and all I could think was please don't cock your leg against it he didn't but walked round it and then continued up the exit isle as we all followed it out to go to the cemetery. He disappeared from view and though we were all laughing about him we assumed that would be the last we would see of him. The next morning we had to go to the solicitors for the will to be read, they had offices in a big Victorian building at the other end of the town from where we were the day before. So you can imagine my amazement when the same little dog came strutting along albeit on the end of a temporary lead, I stopped dead and gestured saying I'm sure that's the little dog from yesterday! The lady with him gave me a funny look and said do you know him and I explained what had happened thinking she was the owner; whilst we were talking he was straining on the lead to go up the path of the solicitors even though we were stood outside the house next door, it gave me goose bumps. The lady sad it wasn't her dog but she found it running around outside her house that was in the next street to the church, she couldn't take it in and leave it in her house as her little dog was on heat, so she grabbed a lead and took it with her, she was on her way to the cemetery to put flowers on her husband's grave as it would have been their anniversary, luckily his grave was very near the gate as you're not allowed to take dogs into the cemetery. So he was at the cemetery at the same time as us and also at the solicitors. I'd like to think it was my nana saying goodbye, I still get goose bumps when I think about it even as I'm writing this.

The months that followed were totally miserable and I think if it wasn't for my little mate Anne I would have gone mad. The bungalow had to be put up for sale, which was fine but my mum wouldn't move out of it and let the estate agents do their job, she insisted on staying and interfering with every prospective sale. I had to clear it out as best as I could with Anne's help and try and make the rather extensive garden look presentable. We were on first name terms with the men at the tip we spent so much time there. As well as that I was up and down to Manchester to look after mums garden and mine, I also had loads of doctors and hospital appointments as my back wasn't getting much chance to recover. I suppose in a way it was fortunate that I was out of work else I'd have been in even more of a pickle. Eventually it was all over and done with and things were able to go back to normal except for a great big hole in my heart.

Barbados

Anne and I still went to as many of the darts venues as we could and a few of our girls from our darts team came to some of them as well so we always had a good laugh. In the Darts World magazine there was an article about a proposed trip to Barbados for a tournament and application forms. I would have dearly loved to go but didn't know if Anne would want to go so far away just for darts and it was expensive as well. I was chatting about it to my mum and she said if Anne would like to go she would treat her for all she had done for us and all the support she'd given me, she also said she would like to come as well though not to play. Anne was over the moon, we was driving everyone mad singing, "Oh were going to Barbados" every time we met. I think we were both a little delirious with the anticipation.

When we went it was everything we could have wished for, beautiful accommodation right on the beach, you could stagger out of bed into the beautiful sea. We were greeted by the Barbadian darts club committee who were lovely (I'm still in touch with one of the ladies to this day). The professionals who went with us were Eric Bristow and Cliff Lazerenko, they both had their wives with them so not everyone was playing so my mum had company when we was. We played in different venues all over the island one was very isolated in the middle of a big field somewhere lovely barbequed food was provided and there was plenty of drink for everyone so a good time was had by all. We didn't just play darts there was plenty of opportunity to do all the usual things a tourist would and we took full benefit of it. We went for a day out on a huge catamaran with wonderful staff, lots of food and drink and a real party atmosphere, mind you it was like that everywhere we went, they are such a laid back nation it would be pretty difficult not to enjoy yourself in their company. I went snorkelling on that trip and had loads of tropical fish feeding from my hand and nibbling my fingers and toes. I also went and swam with the turtles, which was wonderful as well. What a lovely store of memories to have. All too soon it was time to go back home the ten days just flew by.

We loved it so much that we decided to save up and go the next year, my mum didn't join us that time she didn't enjoy the long flight and being deprived of her fags! They say it's not the same if you go back to somewhere you've really enjoyed but I'm pleased to say it was, if not more so as we were greeted like old friends by the wonderful people we'd met before, it felt like putting on a pair of comfy slippers.

Flashback

Out of the blue I received a letter from Jan who lived in Folkstone, I don't know to this day where she got my address from but I was so amazed I forgot I had fallen out with her, (typical me no good at holding a grudge). She said she was living in Manchester now and could we meet up. I rang the number she gave we had a bit of a chat and arranged to meet in the "gay village", I hadn't been going there very much as I was quite happy with my life and circle of friends the way it was.

When I turned up at the bar it was some sort of lesbian meeting, not something I've ever been into and of course the same old Jan as I remember was being the big I am!" Hail fellow," well met and all that but I went along with it and made friends with a few people I may never have met otherwise. As a consequence it led me into going into town more often than I had for a long time. I was also invited to a couple of parties at her girlfriend's home and I managed to talk Ann into coming to those but she hated it with a vengeance when I took her to the gay village with me so that didn't happen very often. I found myself dividing my time between my straight mates and my gay ones.

A couple I made friends with invited me to their home in Longsight for a meal and drinks and because of the driving I was invited to stop for the night, I woke up the next morning to find what I'd thought was a bedding box along the wall was a coffin! Talk about being prepared, I was relieved to find it was empty. The butch one of the partnership was hell bent on having a sex change, she was very young and I did my best to talk her out of it but she was well on the way with the treatment, I've lost track of them now and often wonder what became of her.

<u>OOPS!</u>

One particular night in the club I was frequenting I was sat with two or three couples and feeling slightly left out when from behind me I heard uproarious laughter and turned to see another group of girls having a real giggle mainly at the expense of a little blonde lass that was acting up to it and having a lot of fun. I started talking to them and was enfolded in their company and ended up having a really good night. At the end of which phone numbers were exchanged. I was invited o tea at one of the girls, houses, by the comical little blonde. I turned up and there was the couple whose home it was and Joan, she seemed very excited to see me which did my ego no end of good, I hadn't engendered that reaction in anyone for quite some time. I found out that she lived in Accrington, which was quite a way from where we were but assumed that she was perhaps staying at her friends. Anyway I bit the bullet and invited her to come back and spend the night with me. Her friend the butch one took me to one side and said to go easy with her as she hadn't been on the scene very long and was a bit innocent in some respects, I said I would and off we went. Well we had quite a night of it and she didn't seem at all intimidated or all that naive although we were both a bit nervous at first like you would be with any new relationship. I delivered her back to her friends the next morning and that was the start of a relationship that was to last all of six weeks.

Through these same friends I met another woman from Jersey, she wasn't there all the time but I found myself drawn to her and she did seem to be flirting with me quite a lot. I had mixed feelings about this as I thought she wasn't being very nice to her friend Joan, at the same time it was becoming obvious that Joan was having strong feelings about me, I didn't feel the same and decided I had better end the relationship rather than lead her on. I confided in Doreen and asked her where I should do the deed as I didn't want her driving off somewhere upset and having an accident, she suggested I tell her at her house and that she would be out of the way and turn up later so she wasn't left alone. It was awful, she was so pleased to see me when I arrived and I had to sit her down and tell her it was all over, I felt like I was kicking a puppy. It wasn't as if she'd done anything wrong it just wasn't meant to be. There was a fair amount of tears from both of us but I was very relieved when Doreen turned up and I was able to escape.

Back I went to the nights out with pals. Or should I say so called pals! I was telling Jan and her partner about me splitting up with Joan and she said "oh so you dumped John then did you?" I thought I'd heard wrong and gave her a look to which she responded "I thought you knew", I was flabbergasted and very upset that everyone must have been tittering behind my back. At first I was furious at Joan but when I thought about it when would have been the right time for her to say "by the way I used to be a man"? Bless she was definitely more female than male and must have had a very troubled life because of it. I bumped into her a couple of times in the club after that and tried to talk normally to her and I hope she eventually found someone who would give her the love she deserved.

Rosie

Well I ended up having a fling with the lady from Jersey, which was interesting but not a roses round the door relationship. She was very hard to pin down which I suppose at the time was a bit of a challenge. I was introduced to phone sex! I thought that was a male orientated thing but discovered it could be quite titillating when trying to pursue a long distance relationship, wasn't sure whether I was being led on or not, suppose I was a bit cautious after my last escapade. Anyway it didn't get very far as she seemed to be playing the field although I couldn't prove it but someone did tell me she was on a gay dating site on the internet so I signed up to see if I could catch her out using a false profile. I did have a trip over to Jersey and a good time was had by all so to speak although she did turn out to be a bit too kinky for my taste and we even made a video of the proceedings. I can't say seeing my self cavorting about in the nude was a massive turn on! I think the idea of these things is alright till you see it in the cold light of day. I had taken the camcorder to get footage of Jersey. Mind you it's quite nice to think you are still able to be innocent about some things when you've led the sort of life I have.

One time she said she couldn't manage to get to Manchester for the weekend and asked what I had planned. At the time I had no intentions of going anywhere, a quiet few days were called for. So she said she would ring me and we left it at that. Out of the blue a friend I hadn't seen for ages phoned and asked if we could meet up in the gay village on the Saturday, of course I said yes didn't take a lot of persuading to go for a night out. Anyway we eventually went to the club I used to frequent and who should come strolling in with another woman but Rosie. Her face was a picture when she saw me sitting there, I was fuming, it wasn't as if we had a strong commitment to each other just the fact that I'd been lied to yet again. So in reality it was curtains for that relationship before it even got off the ground. I did see her a couple more times but as far as I was concerned it was just company on a night out.

Fate

Throughout my busy life I always enjoyed quiz shows and game shows both watching and if possible taking part. I had the luck of being on four or five different shows up and down the country as well as quite a few auditions which were enjoyable in their own way, a good way of meeting new people from varying backgrounds and different parts of the country.

I had the opportunity of being in a live lunchtime show that was being held in the studios in Bristol. As I had our Viv in Basingstoke and Chris in Abingdon I decided to make it a bit of a holiday to justify driving all that distance. So spent a happy week in Basingstoke then off to stay with Chris and Alan. He wasn't working at the time so came with me to Bristol to do the show. I didn't win but it's the taking part that matters. After another enjoyable week with them I headed back home.

As always piles of post to plough through most of it destined for the bin, then on to my computer to sort out the junk mail on that. Thought I'd have a look at the gay dating site to see what Rosie had been up to and "lo and behold" there was a message for me! A lady saying she liked the sound of me! Of course I had to have a look at her profile and quite a lot of our interests were similar. I was a Darts player and captain, she was captain of a pool team, we both enjoyed board games and reading, all the usual stuff, plus we were in the same age group which was a bonus. So I responded to her message and as luck would have it she was there to answer it, else I could have probably gone off to do something else and not got back. We were typing messages to each other, well I was typing different messages and the lady in question kept sending me the same one! I asked her if she trusted me to give me her phone number and I would ring her, so she did. We were on the phone for three hours and spent most of it giggling and laughing, we obviously had a similar sense of humour. When she told me she lived in Hayling Island I said I'd just come home from that neck of the woods and went there often. So she said if I was to come down there again we would have to meet up. This first contact was on the 13th of November. We spoke nearly every day sometimes more than once always for a long time, we never seemed short of something to say to each other which was lovely. Anyway I decided we had chatted enough and I would go down and meet her, so I said I was going to Basingstoke again and she said you'll have to come and visit. Little did she know at the time that was my sole reason for going? You have to be a bit wary when you meet someone on the internet, I wasn't nervous but thought she may be.

The plan was I'd stay with my cousin a couple of days and then they were going to Portsmouth so I would follow them down the motorway and they would send me off in the direction of Hayling. I had told Maggie I would ring her as I set off then she would know when to expect me. I hadn't realised she was a bit hard of hearing so when I rang there was no answer and I left a message saying I was on my way. When I arrived on the estate, I took a wrong turning so tried ringing again and she said "are you just setting off?" No I'm already here! I could hear the panic setting in. Anyway I found my way round to her and we had a hug in the garden, then when we got in went to hug and kiss again and our glasses clashed like locked antlers so we took them off. She had a lovely meal ready for me though god knows what it would have been like if I had of been just setting off! After the main meal we were too full up for pudding so left it till later and sat for hours looking at photographs and generally getting to know each other better. Though I felt like I'd come home, as though this is where I should be. We decided it was time to have our desert, it was hysterical we were having pancakes with strawberries and ice cream, the trouble was she'd put it out to soften six hours earlier when we had our meal four litres of liquid ice cream, I'd gathered she was a bit dizzy from some of our conversations and wasn't wrong. It was only when we got over laughing at that that we realized we had been wearing each other's glasses from when I first arrived, a match made in heaven even our eyesight was similar.

We had a lovely weekend together she took me to some of her favourite places, we got on like a house on fire no uncomfortable silences just very relaxed and easy. I was smitten, wasn't sure if she felt the same way but it was early days only two weeks since we first spoke on the phone. Her best friends who had set her up on the site were in Spain and she thought they would go mad at her having a complete stranger staying with her without them around to check me out.

That was the start of many miles of motoring up and down the motorway, eventually my car was nearly doing it on automatic pilot. She worked seventy two hour shifts as a private nurse. So I used to leave as she went to work and come back the day she finished. We couldn't get enough of each other. At Christmas she was spending Christmas day with her sons and my mum was coming to me so I drove down on Boxing Day to take her home with me so she could meet my mum and my friends. She decided to drive so we left my car behind and off we went, it was a horrendous drive as it had been snowing heavily, I didn't realise how brave she was being as she didn't usually drive long distances especially on motorways. We had a nice time and she got on well with my mum and some of my friends we managed to see. Unfortunately by the time we were heading back for the New Year we had both managed to get chest infections. If we had been sensible we would have got back and stayed in but her friends had made arrangements to go to a gay venue for the New Year and talked us in to going as they were curious to meet me I suppose. We were both half dead afterwards but it was an ice breaker with her pals.

When I had been a few times and got my bearings I realised I had been quite near to where Maggie lived a few years previously. I had brought my friend Margaret and her daughter Karen along with my mum on holiday to Southsea. Margaret was a native of Portsmouth and had fond memories of trips on the ferry to Hayling when she was a child, so of course we decided to have a trip down memory lane and off we all went for the ferry. My mum had amazed me by wanting to come on the holiday in the first place as she always said she only wanted to go on holidays abroad and wasn't interested in England, I couldn't quite believe that she wanted to come on a jaunt to Hayling beach either. My instincts were right, she hated sand in her shoes, didn't like walking and both of these were plentiful. We didn't even get far enough to find somewhere to have a cup of tea but fortunately we did find a bus to get us back to the ferry and shut the moaning and groaning up. She said "if I ever see fucking Hayling Island again it will be too soon". So I had been very tongue in cheek when I first met Maggie and told mum where she lived. Each time I came down I used to send her a postcard with greetings from (fucking Hayling Island). I don't think she ever dreamt that I would up sticks and move here.

We were getting on like a house on fire I felt like I'd met my soul mate at long last. I was head over heels in love and knew exactly what I wanted, I think Maggie was a little more cautious than I was but there was plenty of time. The distance was a bit of a problem but I have always enjoyed driving so nothing insurmountable. In the meantime I was getting to know her friends and her sons as well as learning all about each other. One incident was very funny early on in our relationship, we went to her friend's home for a meal, it was the ones that had helped her put her profile on the site we met on so I think they felt a little protective and responsible for her. Whilst Maggie and Dawn were in the kitchen chatting and preparing the meal Sandy was plying me with large whiskeys and grilling me about my finances and intentions. I was hard put to keep my face straight she was acting like Maggie's father, did I own my own house, had I any savings, was I in debt, what was I likely to do? Would I be moving down south, things we hadn't at the time talked about ourselves. Maggie's face was a picture when I told her about it later she was mortified, I didn't mind one little bit as they were only looking out for their friend how could you be offended by that?

The periods of going back home were getting more difficult for both of us, Maggie felt left out when I went back to basically what had been my life before we met and she was at work so something had to give. I said I was quite happy to give up my home and move in with her if she wanted me to, she was much more cautious and frightened of me giving up my home and things not working out. So as I was in a council house I put myself on the transfer list not holding out much hope as I couldn't imagine anyone wanting to leave Hayling or the surrounding area to live in Salford. I only had one person who was slightly interested and funnily enough she was gay as well. Her house was a bit of a shambles but with distinct possibilities, she travelled up to have a look at mine and was excited about the closeness of the gay village. Her suggestion that we house share so she could use mine as a weekend destination for jaunts in the gay community left me cold so it all came to nothing. Eventually I convinced Maggie I wasn't worried about giving up my home in the least, wherever she was would be home to me. So the decision was made and everything was packed up, sold up or given away, Chris came and helped with the packing and so on and that was it, farewell to Swinton and hello to my new life.

Obviously I wasn't completely done with Manchester as my mum was still there so I went back and forth every three weeks to sort out her washing and cleaning and shopping and anything else she wanted. She also seemed quite settled to the idea of me going south again even if it was to Hayling and she did come and stay with us so I think she decided it wasn't so bad after all so long as she didn't have to go to the beach! Also she got to meet Maggie's boys and her eldest was thrilled to bits to have a new Gran though not sure if he classed her as grandma or granddad as even though she was getting on she was still very butch in her demeanour and dress.

We slotted in with each other very well, Maggie loves gardening and decorating and I am always happy in the kitchen so we didn't end up getting on each other's nerves as can happen with two women in the same household we actually complemented each other.

One of the sad things about Maggie and I getting together was I lost my pal little Ann, I don't really know why as they met each other and got on really well but when the reality of me moving permanently presented itself she went off on one, I couldn't understand it as we had been such good pals and had many adventures together but she just wouldn't have it and we fell out. She wouldn't even look on us as an extra holiday destination and given we'd travelled far and wide together in the past I thought she'd enjoy it and we would keep in touch. It wasn't to be and I didn't see her again till my mum's funeral.

I used to go to pool with Maggie and even had a try when they were short of players but it wasn't for me I was completely useless. Unfortunately the darts leagues were on the same night as the pool and though I had the opportunity of playing for a couple of different pubs the hassle of me being in one part of Portsmouth and Maggie in another didn't add up and I would have probably spent more time being lost than playing. Also I wouldn't have been able to have a drink like I could when I played locally in Swinton as everything was within staggering distance. So I became a pool spectator instead, but it was a good way to meet all Maggie's other friends.

<u>Quiz</u>

When the opportunity to try for a chance of getting on Deal or No Deal I jumped at the chance and whilst I was applying for the forms I put Maggie's name in as well. She was horrified when I told her but comforted with the fact that we'd be lucky if we even got an audition she let me carry on. In due course the application forms arrived and I filled them in for both of us. The upshot was Maggie was called for an audition and I wasn't ironical to say the least.

It coincided with my mum being on holiday with us so off we went to Bristol. It was at a big hotel and there were hundreds of people there so it allayed her nerves a little when she realised they were all in the same boat. When she had her audition she came out saying she thought she'd blown it as she hadn't realised it was being recorded went in to panic when they told her. I was quite convinced it would have the opposite effect from what she told me, they probably thought they had a female Norman Wisdom on their hands as she can be very comical without even trying. They said not to sit worrying about it as thousands of people up and down the country had auditions and just to forget about unless they phoned. So she did, then they rang weeks later and panic mode was back on!

The day before we were to leave was spent with all the primping and girly things that feminine ladies do. The hairstyle changed about six times, different colours of nail varnish appeared and then vanished. Eventually it was bedtime and I didn't expect her to have a good night but I had to as I would be driving. I woke out of a deep sleep to a pitiful cry coming through the bedroom window, I staggered up and opened the window to be confronted by what looked like the creature from the black lagoon! The beautiful hairstyle had gone and was replaced by droopy bangs at the side looking like spaniel ears and covered in very smelly pond weed. When I'd stopped laughing and got her in she told me she was trying to rescue her Koi carp that had become tangled in the netting, over reached and went in head first. It was lucky she hadn't banged her head on the rocks she could have drowned without me knowing, I wouldn't even have looked out there at five in the morning! I helped her get sorted out and calmed her down then off we went. Maggie was going to navigate as there seemed to be an awful lot of roundabouts to negotiate on the way but before we had gone very far she was fast asleep. She suddenly came to as I was going round one of the roundabouts and thought I'd taken a wrong turning, she was about twenty too late we were nearly at our destination.

It was all very exciting getting settled in and meeting all the other competitors and their friends and families old and new that time passed really quickly. Without going into all the details we spent full days at the studio, even the friends and family had to rehearse while waiting for the shows to come on. We were informed we were going to be there for a week then they would break for three months and back we would go, the magic of television, so long as you didn't get pregnant die your hair or put on weight or lose it you was all right. Maggie started recording her shows about half way through the week. Then before we knew it we were on our way back home. We were told not to tell people how it all worked or what the results were as it would have spoiled it for when the different shows were aired. That was a big shame from my point of view as my mum became ill and passed away before we went back and she'd been so excited for us but never got to know how it was going.

So to another sad part of my life mixed in with all my happiness, my mum must have been suffering for a long time without letting on because from her ringing me to say she was ill and me going up to her, she was diagnosed with cancer and only lasted three weeks. I didn't even get to say goodbye, they had let her go home with a huge care package set up, we had to come home but they said it would be fine and it was the best way for the care package to get in motion, the senior nurse rang me to say everything was fine after the first night on her own. I spoke to her twice the next day and she seemed reasonably chirpy for someone doped up on morphine. Then the next morning I rang and a carer answered the phone and said an ambulance was taking her back to the hospital as they'd found her draped over the bed unable to get back in, they obviously didn't lower it for her. Anyway I talked to the nurse at the hospital, we'd got to know the staff pretty well and she said mum didn't want to be back there and was no longer interested in even talking to anyone. I had a call the next morning to get there, so rang our Chris as she was closer and she set off. When I rang half way there to see if she was still with us she was. Chris told her I'd rang and was nearly there she said "I've had enough, I'm off now" and died. Chris couldn't credit it thought she was asleep. Our family obviously don't do lingering deaths.

Shortly after we were due in Bristol to continue with the show, turned out a good way to help with the grief. We used to travel by coach to the studio every morning and there was always singing involved, in our particular group that arrived together we had a young man with a cheeky smile and a lovely voice, after we discovered him nobody else volunteered. We decided he was on the wrong show, should have been X factor!

Two weeks and twenty one shows passed by in a flash and all of a sudden it was Maggie's turn, you have no idea as to when it's going to be your turn so it's all very exciting. The box she had was number ten and I took this as a good omen, my birthday date so I was quite convinced my mum was watching over us. Her first offer was six thousand pounds and it went from bad to worse from that moment on. She completely decimated the red side of the board and when she was at the last five boxes she had four blue and one red with a hundred thousand in it. By this time I was down there with her for a bit of moral support, the banker offered four thousand for the box, which was the second best offer of the game. My Maggie isn't a gambler and she asked me what to do? The only advice I could offer was don't regret it whatever you decide. She thought for a long time and I was quite sure she was going to accept then she told Noel she was ready and flabbergasted us all by saying no deal! Then went on to open three blue boxes one after the other, everyone including me thought she'd been very brave to chance it. The next offer was for twenty-two thousand pounds, the remaining boxes had either fifty pounds or the hundred thousand pounds. All along I'd been convinced it was a good box just because it was my birthday date but I was amazed when Maggie considered the offer for a long time again before accepting the deal. Her box contained the hundred thousand when it was opened but we were very happy with what she'd won. It was an experience of a lifetime and we were able to start our retirement debt free with no huge problems.

Our present to ourselves was two little Pomeranian pups, litter twins who we love dearly and would be company for Poppy, We called them Nip and Tuck as after buying them we couldn't afford a face lift even if we wanted one.

Oh yes, the added extra was that our young man who sang to us every day, didn't do well on the show at all but a couple of years later came second on X factor and hasn't looked back. Well done Olly Murs, we think of you often.

Contentment

My life has meandered through many different paths with lots of twists and turns. Some happy some sad, lots of the time funny, but I believe all leading to where I am now. With my soul-mate. We are opposites in so many ways but still manage to complement each other. We gave up our hobbies of pool and darts and have taken up lawn bowling as a sport we can do together and we absolutely love it, granted we aren't always playing in the same place at the same time but it is a shared hobby. We have met lots of lovely people nearly like having an extra family. I somehow managed to become Club President in my third season, anyone that knew me in my very chequered past would never have expected that, including me and though I embarked on it with much trepidation in the end I thoroughly enjoyed it.

I started my life in one seaside resorted and am likely to end it in another and I couldn't be happier about it.

From sorrow to happiness with much in between.